T0348702

Navigating the Product Galaxy

A Practical Handbook for Product Managers

Michele Galli

Apress®

Navigating the Product Galaxy: A Practical Handbook for Product Managers

Michele Galli
London, UK

ISBN-13 (pbk): 979-8-8688-1147-0   ISBN-13 (electronic): 979-8-8688-1148-7
https://doi.org/10.1007/979-8-8688-1148-7

Managing Director, Apress Media LLC: Welmoed Spahr
Acquisitions Editor: James Robinson Prior
Development Editor: James Markham
Coordinating Editor: Gryffin Winkler

Cover designed by eStudioCalamar

Distributed to the book trade worldwide by Springer Science+Business Media New York, 233 Spring Street, 6th Floor, New York, NY 10013. Phone 1-800-SPRINGER, fax (201) 348-4505, e-mail orders-ny@springer-sbm.com, or visit www.springeronline.com. Apress Media, LLC is a California LLC and the sole member (owner) is Springer Science + Business Media Finance Inc (SSBM Finance Inc). SSBM Finance Inc is a **Delaware** corporation.

For information on translations, please e-mail booktranslations@springernature.com; for reprint, paperback, or audio rights, please e-mail bookpermissions@springernature.com.

Apress titles may be purchased in bulk for academic, corporate, or promotional use. eBook versions and licenses are also available for most titles. For more information, reference our Print and eBook Bulk Sales web page at http://www.apress.com/bulk-sales.

Any source code or other supplementary material referenced by the author in this book can be found here: https://www.apress.com/gp/services/source-code.

If disposing of this product, please recycle the paper

To my wife, Clementina.
You are my sunshine when skies are gray.

Table of Contents

About the Author

Michele Galli is a product management expert with over a decade of experience across various sectors, including fintech, prop-tech, and the Internet of Things. His entrepreneurial journey began as the founder and CEO of an IoT startup, where he refined his skills in building innovative products and navigating complex markets. Currently, Michele leads the onboarding and growth functions at Wise, a globally recognized money platform, as Product Director. His role at Wise involves acquiring new customers, streamlining onboarding processes for both individual and business clients, and ensuring sustainable growth for one of the biggest fintech companies in the world.

About the Technical Reviewer

Ari Aparikyan is a Director of Engineering at Wise. After graduating from the University of Oxford with a Computer Science degree, he joined Wise as a product engineer, where he worked at the intersection of product and software development across multiple teams during his tenure—along with a year-long stint at Intuit Quickbooks as an Engineering Manager.

Acknowledgments

First and foremost, I want to thank my wife, Clementina. Your support, through both the stressful moments and the calm ones, has given me the time and space to learn the hard lessons that fill this book. You have been my rock through every challenge, and I am who I am today, in no small part, because of you. Your love, wisdom, and patience have taught me how to be more sensitive, how to truly listen, and how to stay grounded, even when the world feels overwhelming. Without your encouragement, patience, and belief in me, this journey would have been far more difficult, and for that, I am forever grateful.

A special thanks to my family, friends, colleagues, and the many industry experts who took the time to review and provide feedback on this book. Your insights and constructive critiques helped shape and improve it in ways I could not have achieved alone. This book is better because of your input, thank you!

Introduction

Welcome to *Navigating the Product Galaxy*, a book created as a handbook for aspiring and seasoned product managers who want to shape the future through innovation, strategy, and a firm focus on customers.

As you read this book, you will learn how to navigate the challenges of product management, with insights from real-world experiences, to create successful products in any industry. Whether you're managing a software development team or leading a marketing campaign for a new line of gourmet chocolates, the core skills of understanding customer needs, coordinating cross-functional teams, and driving product success remain the same.

The knowledge in this book doesn't come from theory alone—it's the result of many years spent in product management. As a founder of a startup, I've faced the challenges of building something from the ground up. My time working in other startups taught me the importance of deeply understanding customers to guide product decisions, especially when having a limited customer base. In these environments, where you often make big bets with limited data, I learned how to take calculated risks and focus on the key product metrics that drive user engagement and satisfaction.

Transitioning from startups to larger, hyper-growth companies presented a new set of challenges for me and my teams. Working in these companies has shown me the pace at which decisions must be made and the importance of getting things right as quickly as possible. I also learned the ability to manage cross-functional teams at a much larger scale and how to balance short-term demands with long-term strategic goals, making sure that rapid growth doesn't come at the expense of the product's core values or user experience.

During these years, I've had the privilege of working alongside some of the best product managers, leaders, and advisors in the tech industry, as well as learning from experienced investors. Their insights and guidance have been incredibly valuable in shaping my approach to product management.

Now, as a product director in a company with an exceptional product and user-centric culture, I continue to refine and apply these lessons. I don't claim to have all the answers, but my goal is to share with you the hard-earned lessons and real-world experiences that have shaped my journey and give you a real edge in the field. This isn't everything there is to know about product management, but what you'll find here will give you an advantage over most other product managers out there.

Navigating the Product Galaxy covers seven key topics, each an essential aspect of product management. From the foundational principles that ground you in your role to the strategies that push you into the future, this guide shows you the path at every turn. It's a path that explores the nature of product management, embraces the dual roles of leader and collaborator, and balances the triangle of market needs, technology, and business objectives.

At the heart of this journey is the customer. Encouraging a customer-centric strategy is your mission, guiding every decision, from the arcs of your product's design to the details of its features. It's a mission that challenges you to listen, empathize, and innovate, so that the customer finds value, delight, and a sense of belonging.

In creating this guide, I've drawn inspiration from the pioneers of product management and the latest thought leaders who have brought remarkable products to life and who continue to push the boundaries of what's possible.

But more than anything, this book is a reflection of you—the aspiring product manager eager to make your mark, the seasoned professional seeking to refine your art, and the visionary leader driven to create products that inspire, empower, and transform.

By the end of this book, you will have the knowledge and skills to become an exceptional product manager, to create and implement inspiring product strategies, lead and collaborate with cross-functional teams, understand and use key product metrics, and stay current with industry trends and new technologies. Whether you're developing the next groundbreaking app or leading a product team, this book is here to support your journey.

Chapter 1: Introduction to Product Management

Discover the essence of product management, its evolution, and why it's so important in today's tech-driven world. By the end of this chapter, you'll have a solid understanding of the foundational principles that every product manager needs to follow.

Chapter 2: Strategy Development

Learn how to create an inspiring vision and strategy for your product and how to set actionable goals, analyze your market, and outmaneuver your competition. This chapter will teach you the skills to create roadmaps that guide your product with clear purpose and ambitious planning.

Chapter 3: Stakeholder Management

Master the art of communication and relationship building. This chapter prepares you to effectively engage with internal and external teams and use feedback to shape your product's direction.

Chapter 4: User Research and Product Metrics

Put customers at the heart of your product decisions. By the end of this chapter, you'll know how to conduct effective user research, select the right KPIs, and use both qualitative and quantitative analyses to make informed, data-driven decisions that drive user engagement.

Chapter 5: Go-to-Market and Product Launch

This chapter will guide you through creating a successful launch plan and managing post-launch phases. You'll have the tools to iterate and innovate continuously and make your product thrive in the market.

Chapter 6: Team Leadership, Collaboration, and Ethical Considerations

Learn how to lead and inspire your product team while cultivating a collaborative and ethical culture. Discover how to balance leadership and teamwork, unite cross-functional teams, and uphold ethical standards in every aspect of your product management.

Chapter 7: Current and Future Trends in Product Management

Prepare for the future by exploring the latest trends and emerging opportunities in product management. This chapter challenges you to think ahead, adapt to new methodologies, and lead the development of products that will shape the future of the tech industry.

CHAPTER 1

Introduction to Product Management

Product management is the journey of transforming an idea into a successful product. It's a discipline that demands creativity, strategic thinking, and effective execution to navigate the entire product life cycle.

Product managers are the orchestrators of this journey, acting as leaders who understand needs, navigate through market and technological changes, and inspire teams to turn vision into reality. Some of the most significant lessons I've learned on this journey came from keeping the team inspired and aligned with the vision while also staying grounded in the practicalities of execution—and you will learn them too as you go through this book.

The role of a product manager is complex and requires a balance between conviction and collaboration. PMs are tasked with guiding cross-functional teams through the product development life cycle, so that every phase, from conception to launch, is executed in the right way. They must have the ability to lead with authority, conviction, and vision, while also supporting an environment of collaboration and mutual respect among diverse teams. Early in my career, I learned that cultivating this environment of respect can help unlock the full potential of cross-functional teams. It's not always easy, but it's really important for the success of the product.

© Michele Galli 2025
M. Galli, *Navigating the Product Galaxy*, https://doi.org/10.1007/979-8-8688-1148-7_1

Product managers serve as the bridge between the market's needs and the company's goals to make the products meet and exceed customer expectations. For this reason, they must have their fingers on the pulse of the market, understand customer needs and trends, and also keep on top of the latest technological innovations.

Every PM must have a customer-centric approach. This principle places user needs and experiences at the front of every decision, from the initial design stages through to post-launch improvements. PMs need to empathize with the users, understand their pain points, and create products that provide real value and solutions to their problems. But understanding these pain points is not as straightforward as it may seem. There were times when I thought I knew what the users needed, only to realize later that I had missed a key pain point. It's a humbling experience as it reinforces the importance of user engagement and empathy. It's equally important to remember the distinction between what users *want* and what they actually *need*. Sometimes users may ask for specific features or solutions based on their current experiences, but as product managers, we need to see beyond that and anticipate their future needs as well. Understanding this gap between "want" and "need" helps develop products that truly resonate with users.

Sometimes PMs are called mini-CEOs because of the broad scope of their role. But while the PM plays a key role in steering the product development and aligning team efforts, it's important to remember that the CEO sets the vision and strategic direction of the company. The PM translates this vision into actionable plans and coordinates with various teams to ensure the product's success. I've seen how critical this translation process is—when done well, it turns a broad company vision into something tangible and actionable for the team. When it's lacking, however, it can lead to lots of missed opportunities. This collaboration ensures that the CEO's goals are realized through the product's journey from concept to market.

The CEO is the face of the company, representing it to investors and stakeholders, and bearing the ultimate responsibility for the company's performance. The PM, on the other hand, focuses on the product, making sure it meets market demands and aligns with the company's strategy. Unlike a CEO, who oversees the entire organization, the PM's scope is narrower but nonetheless important and deeply involved in the day-to-day operations related to the product.

In this chapter, we explore these key principles, setting the stage for a deeper understanding of the role and its significance in the tech industry:

1. **The Product Management Life Cycle:**
   Navigate the entire journey of product management, from initial ideation to successful launch and continuous evolution.

2. **Leadership and Collaboration in Product Development:**
   Master the dual role of a product manager as both a leader and a collaborator. Learn how to inspire your team and to drive product excellence.

3. **Balancing Market Needs with Tech and Business Goals:**
   Balance the demands of the market with technology and business objectives. Learn how to align these forces to create products that meet market needs while driving business success.

4. **Encouraging a User-Centric Product Strategy:**
   Adopt a customer-first mindset that places user needs at the core of your product strategy. Develop the skills to ensure that every product decision enhances user satisfaction and engagement.

5. **Embracing Adaptability in Product Management:**
   Thrive in the face of change and uncertainty. Learn
   how to quickly adapt your products and strategies
   as new information arises, keeping your product
   relevant and competitive.

The Product Management Life Cycle

The product life cycle is not linear but a dynamic process that requires
a mix of vision and relentless focus on the users. The key phases are the
ideation phase, the design and development phase, the launch phase, and
the post-launch learning phase.

Ideation Phase

The ideation phase is the starting point of the product management
process, where the seeds of innovation are developed. In this phase, you
must first identify and clearly define the problem you're aiming to solve.
One of the biggest mistakes I see in product teams is jumping to solutions
too quickly without fully understanding the problem. By taking the time
to build confidence that the problem exists and is the right one to solve,
you set a strong foundation for the entire process. We will explore how to
effectively build this confidence in Chapter 4, which will provide deeper
insights into techniques and methodologies for ensuring you're solving the
right problem.

Going back to the ideation phase, you'll collect inputs from different
sources to develop initial concepts. Your goal is to identify and articulate
opportunities that align with both user needs and business objectives,
laying the groundwork for a successful product.

To navigate this phase effectively, product managers can use a variety of techniques and approaches, such as brainstorming sessions, which provide an environment for team members to freely share ideas. These sessions can be structured around specific challenges, supporting participants to think outside the box and consider a wide range of potential solutions. Techniques like SCAMPER (Substitute, Combine, Adapt, Modify, Put to another use, Eliminate, and Reverse) can also stimulate creative thinking, pushing teams to explore ideas from different angles.

Applying SCAMPER in Real Life

Imagine you're working on developing a new feature for a fitness tracking app, here's how you could use SCAMPER:

- **Substitute:** What if we substitute text notifications with push notifications to keep users more engaged with their daily fitness goals?

- **Combine:** Can we combine the fitness tracking feature with a social sharing option to improve user engagement and create a sense of community?

- **Adapt:** How can we adapt the swipe functionality from popular dating apps to our navigation process, making it easier for users to log their workouts?

- **Modify:** What if we modify the color scheme to make it more accessible for color-blind users?

- **Put to another use:** Can we repurpose our chat feature to provide personalized fitness tips and customer support?

- **Eliminate:** What if we eliminate the login requirement to reduce user friction?

- **Reverse:** Can we reverse the onboarding process to allow users to explore the app before signing up?

Another important aspect of the ideation phase is market research. PMs need to understand the competitive landscape, trends, and unmet user needs to identify opportunities that are both innovative and viable. Tools like the SWOT analysis (Strengths, Weaknesses, Opportunities, Threats) can help product managers assess potential ideas in the context of the market and the company's capabilities, helping in the selection of concepts that have the best chance of success.

User research plays the most important role in this phase. As a PM, you should engage with potential users through interviews, surveys, and observation to uncover insights into their pain points and behaviors which then inform the development of user personas and journey maps, with a detailed understanding of the target audience and how they might interact with your product.

Quantitative analysis is incredibly valuable here, as it can reveal patterns, behaviors, and segmentation within the existing customer data and help focus qualitative research, making interviews and surveys more effective.

Once a range of ideas has been generated, product managers must evaluate and prioritize them to determine which are worth pursuing further. It's important to focus on understanding the problems at this stage, rather than jumping to solutions too soon. Only after you and your team have a crystal-clear understanding of the problem should you begin brainstorming solutions so that the solutions developed are truly addressing the right challenges.

You can use techniques like the Value Proposition Canvas to help clarify how an idea delivers value to users and the business. Prioritization frameworks, such as RICE (Reach, Impact, Confidence, Effort) or the Kano Model, can also help assess the potential impact and feasibility of each concept, to make sure resources are used on the most promising opportunities.

Throughout the ideation phase, product managers should create an environment where team members feel empowered to contribute ideas and feedback, recognizing that great concepts can come from anywhere.

Value Proposition Canvas

The value proposition canvas is a tool used to ensure that a product or service is positioned around what the customer values and needs. It helps businesses understand their customers better and align their products or services accordingly. The canvas consists of two main sections: the customer profile and the value map.

Customer Profile

This section helps you clarify your customer segment and It includes three components:

Customer jobs:

- Functional jobs: Tasks or problems the customer needs to solve.

- Social jobs: How customers want to be perceived by others.

- Emotional jobs: Emotional states customers want to achieve or avoid.

Pains:

- Challenges or negative experiences customers face while trying to accomplish their jobs.

- Risks or potential negative outcomes they want to avoid.

Gains:

- Desired benefits and positive outcomes.

- Ways customers measure success and satisfaction.

Value Map

This section helps you describe how your product or service creates value for the customer and It includes three components:

Products and services:

- List of all the products and services you offer to help your customer get their jobs done.

Pain relievers:

- How your products or services alleviate customer pains.

- Specific features that help reduce or eliminate these challenges.

Gain creators:

- How your products or services provide customer gains.

- Features that help achieve the desired benefits and positive outcomes.

Design and Development Phase

From the ideation phase, we transition to the design and development phase, where abstract ideas begin to take tangible form. This phase is a blend of creativity and user-centric focus that needs collaboration between designers, analysts, product analytics, developers, and product managers to make the initial concept a functional, market-ready product.

Design translates the insights collected during ideation into user-centric designs by creating user interfaces that are intuitive and engaging. Using wireframes and prototypes, designers and product managers can visualize and test different design concepts, iterating based on user feedback to refine their product's usability.

Techniques such as Design Thinking (Figure 1-1) emphasize empathy with users, starting with the "Empathize" step, pushing teams to explore a wide range of solutions and to view challenges from the user's perspective. These steps can be done through design sprints, which are time-boxed sessions that allow teams to rapidly prototype and test ideas, providing the necessary insights in a short period.

Figure 1-1. *Design thinking*

The development phase often overlaps with the design process. While designers are focused on creating and refining the user interface, developers can begin working on foundational elements that don't require finalized designs. For example, they can set up the project's architecture, databases, and backend services, while other aspects of development should wait for the final designs to avoid misalignment. Engineers and designers must work closely together to prevent silos.

In the early stages of the design process, engineering may scope the project to understand the technical feasibility and make sure the designs are achievable within the project's technical limits. Involving engineering early also helps de-risk the biggest technical unknowns, allowing the team to speed up execution by identifying which parts can be parallelized and which should be front-loaded for faster development.

Breaking down the development process into manageable sprints, typically one to two weeks in length, allows teams to focus on delivering specific features or functionalities and enables continuous testing, feedback, and improvement. Practices like Continuous Integration/Continuous Deployment (CI/CD) automate testing and deployment processes, making sure changes are integrated and the product remains in a releasable state throughout development. For more on CI/CD, I recommend three excellent books: *Continuous Delivery* by Jez Humble and David Farley, *The DevOps Handbook* by Gene Kim, Patrick Debois, John Willis, and Jez Humble, and *Continuous Integration* by Paul M. Duvall, Steve Matyas, and Andrew Glover.

Another component of the design and development phase is user testing, as it provides feedback on the product's functionality, usability, and overall user experience. Usability studies and A/B testing allow teams to collect insights directly from users, informing decisions about designs and features, and identifying potential issues early in the development process, reducing the risk of costly changes down the line. These concepts will be covered in more detail in Chapter 4.

Throughout this phase, you should always maintain a user-centric approach by actively listening to user feedback. Focus on understanding their pain points and struggles, and be ready to iterate on the product based on this input. It's quite important to stay open to feedback during this time and be willing to pivot if users indicate that a solution isn't effective as this feedback often makes the difference between a good product and a great one.

Launch Phase

The launch phase is the culmination of planning, design, and development efforts, marking the moment when the product is introduced to the market. During this phase, you will coordinate with marketing, sales, customer support, analytics, and tech, to ensure a smooth transition from development to user adoption.

As the launch date approaches, product managers must ensure that all elements of the go-to-market strategy are executed, including finalizing marketing materials, press releases, and launch campaigns that highlight the product's unique value proposition and benefits to the target audience.

Simultaneously, PMs must collaborate with the sales team to equip them with the knowledge and tools they need to effectively sell the product like training sessions, product demos, and sales materials that detail the product's features, competitive advantages, and use cases.

Product managers must also work closely with customer support teams to develop FAQs, troubleshooting guides, and support protocols to help address user questions and issues, creating positive early experiences with the product.

After launch, monitor and respond to user feedback. Product managers should make sure mechanisms are in place for collecting user feedback, reviews, and usage data. This should be a collaborative effort with analysts and user researchers in the team to help identify and address any unexpected issues or areas for improvement.

Continuous Learning

In product, you must cultivate a mindset of curiosity and openness to new ideas and perspectives. Product managers, along with their teams, are pushed to seek out learning opportunities in different forms, whether through formal education, such as workshops and courses, or through informal channels like podcasts, blogs, and industry events. This allows them to explore a wide range of topics relevant to product management, including emerging technologies, user experience design, market research techniques, and leadership skills.

For example, consider following industry leaders on platforms like LinkedIn, subscribing to product management podcasts and blogs. One of the podcasts that I find particularly valuable is *Lenny's Podcast*, where Lenny Rachitsky dives deep into real-world product challenges with experienced guests. *The Product Podcast* is another excellent resource that offers a variety of perspectives on product management practices. When it comes to blogs, *Mind the Product* offers good practical advice, while *Product Coalition* offers a community-driven approach. These resources help PMs stay connected with the broader product management community and keep product skills sharp.

To stay on top of tech, *TechCrunch* and *Wired* are good reads. These publications can help you understand how new technologies can be used to improve products.

Equally important is the understanding of consumer behaviors and market trends. As preferences and behaviors evolve, product managers must be skilled at identifying changes in the market and anticipating how these changes could impact their product strategy. This requires the analysis of market research and user data and also engaging directly with users through interviews, surveys, and feedback channels to get insights into their needs and expectations. I recommend conducting some level of market research analysis at least every one to two quarters to stay aligned with market shifts.

Another component is the development of soft skills, such as leadership, communication, and empathy. Effective product managers rely heavily on the ability to lead cross-functional teams (especially without formal authority), communicate vision and strategy, and empathize with users and team members. Developing these skills can improve collaboration, encourage a positive work culture, and ultimately lead to the development of products that truly resonate with users. If you want to go deeper into improving these skills, I recommend reading books like *Leaders Eat Last* by Simon Sinek and *Crucial Conversations* by Al Switzler, Joseph Grenny, and Ron McMillan.

Leadership and Collaboration in Product Development

Product managers must balance leadership and collaboration to succeed in their roles of both visionaries and team players. Effective leaders should create an environment where ideas, expertise, and skills from diverse domains converge to create innovative products.

Representing Visionary Leadership

PMs are required to articulate a clear, convincing vision for the product, which serves as the north star for the team, guiding every decision, from design and development to marketing and sales. This requires a deep understanding of the market, the users, and the unique value proposition of the product, translated into a roadmap that aligns with the organization's goals. As a leader, the product manager must ensure that this vision is communicated clearly and embraced by every team member. From what I have seen, one of the most common challenges found by product managers is ensuring that their vision doesn't get diluted as it moves across different teams and, to avoid this, PMs should keep reinforcing the vision at every opportunity they have to maintain alignment.

To effectively express this leadership, a product manager must be forward-thinking, scanning the horizon for emerging trends and opportunities that align with the product's long-term goals, which enables them to anticipate changes in the market and adapt the product strategy accordingly, keeping the product relevant and competitive. Being proactive in this way helps keep the product ahead of the curve and also inspires confidence within the team, knowing that we're preparing for future challenges.

A key aspect of the PM's leadership is the ability to translate complex ideas into a clear and actionable roadmap by breaking down the vision into specific, measurable objectives that guide the team's efforts. It's about making the vision achievable, providing a clear path forward while also allowing for flexibility to adapt to changes along the way. We will expand on these concepts in Chapter 2.

It also means being an effective storyteller as a product manager must be able to articulate the product vision in a way that excites and motivates the team, stakeholders, and customers, involving actions that consistently reinforce the vision's value. In meetings, linking discussions back to the vision helps keep everyone on track and ensures that even small decisions contribute to the larger goal. In one-on-one interactions, the PM should listen to team members' ideas and feedback, integrating these contributions into the broader narrative of the product's journey, to keep the vision in everyone's mind and create a shared sense of purpose.

PMs should also build trust through transparency, integrity, and by demonstrating commitment to the team. A visionary leader listens to feedback, acknowledges challenges, and works collaboratively to overcome obstacles, showing that they are invested in the team's success and the realization of the product vision. Early in my career, I learned that transparency, especially in challenging times, builds long-term trust, which is fundamental for navigating difficult phases of product development.

Finally, visionary leaders must demonstrate resilience by bringing a vision to life in a journey filled with uncertainties and remain loyal in their commitment to the vision, inspiring the team to stay focused on the ultimate goal.

Being Hands-on

Among all the signals and behaviors that identify great product managers, being hands-on is, in my experience, the most telling. Successful product managers are not just facilitators; they must be doers. While they don't necessarily need to be skilled coders, great designers, or analysts, they should be capable of stepping into these roles if needed. If any of these functions are missing or underperforming, a great product manager should step in to prevent the team from getting stuck. I've had many instances where stepping in to fill a temporary gap kept the project moving forward, and it also showed the team that I'm willing to support them in any way necessary.

Acting in this way allows the product manager to understand the product and contribute to its development in a tangible way. It also helps keep a high quality bar in every department as the PM can better judge the work of each function. What I've found is, when the team sees you actively involved, it boosts morale and creates a stronger collaborative spirit. Being hands-on also helps build credibility within the team, as the product manager demonstrates their ability to tackle challenges alongside their team members.

To be effectively hands-on, consider doing any of these:

- Invest time in learning the fundamentals of coding, design, and data analysis. Online courses, tutorials, and workshops can provide a good foundation.

- Spend time with different team members to understand their processes and understand how different functions contribute to the product.

- Take on smaller tasks in coding, design, or analysis to improve your understanding and show your team that you're willing to get your hands dirty.

- Hold regular meetings with each function to stay updated on their progress and offer help where needed.

- Familiarize yourself with the tools your team uses. This can help you provide better support and feedback.

- When issues arise, participate in troubleshooting sessions as your involvement can help the team find solutions more quickly and effectively.

Inspiring a Culture of Collaboration

Collaboration is the lifeblood of successful products and product managers must cultivate an environment where open communication, mutual respect, and cross-functional teamwork are the norms by breaking down silos between departments and facilitating cross-disciplinary meetings to keep everyone updated on progress and challenges. From what I've seen during the years, some of the best ideas come from these collaborative settings, where team members feel comfortable sharing their thoughts and expertise without fear of judgment.

Teams should be empowered to share feedback openly in regular cross-functional meetings, where team members can update each other on their progress, discuss any obstacles they're facing, and brainstorm solutions together. These meetings should be structured to promote openness and inclusivity and ensure that all voices are heard to help identify potential issues early and leverage the expertise of the team to solve problems more creatively and efficiently.

I've learned that encouraging team members to step into each other's shoes can create greater empathy and understanding across roles. As a PM, you should encourage team members to understand the challenges of different roles and promote empathy. One way to do this is through shadowing sessions, where team members spend time working alongside colleagues from different functions.

Product managers play an important role in harmonizing the different perspectives within the team by promoting a culture where feedback is sought, received, and acted upon constructively. A lesson I've taken to heart is the importance of acting on feedback. When the team sees that their input leads to tangible changes, it builds trust and encourages more open communication.

Create opportunities for informal interactions and team-building activities to build trust and personal connections among team members, and celebrate successes, whether they be major milestones or small wins, to reinforce the team's sense of unity and shared purpose.

Navigating Cross-functional Dynamics

Designers, analysts, researchers, engineers, marketers, and sales teams all bring valuable but sometimes divergent views to the table which will require you to balance these to maintain focus on the user's needs with diplomatic skill and the ability to find common ground. Successful product managers are expert at leveraging the strengths of each discipline, so that all voices are heard and that the final product reflects a synthesis of the team's collective expertise.

PMs must excel in translating the product vision into terms that resonate with each team member, whether it's discussing the user experience with UI/UX designers, data with product analysts, technical requirements with developers, or market positioning with the marketing team. You need to speak the language of each discipline, understanding their challenges, and articulating how their contributions fit into the broader product strategy.

Conflict resolution is another key aspect here as differences in priorities, perspectives, or approaches are inevitable when multiple teams collaborate. Product managers must be experts at identifying the root causes of conflicts and facilitating constructive discussions to find mutually acceptable solutions which sometimes means finding creative ways to align different goals without compromising the product's integrity.

Product managers can also create a sense of responsibility among team members by delegating ownership, which makes teams feel more invested in the product's success and more willing to contribute their best ideas and efforts. Through my experience, I've learned that when teams have ownership over their work, they're more engaged, which in return leads to better results.

Finally, recognize the contributions of all teams, not just in terms of successful outcomes but also the efforts and challenges overcome along the way to build a stronger, more cohesive working relationship between the various functions involved in product development.

Leadership Styles

The nature of product development often needs different leadership styles at different stages of the process. From coaching and mentoring during the ideation phase to more directive leadership when making tough decisions under tight deadlines, the ability to adapt one's leadership style is important to navigating the product life cycle. Product managers must be sensitive to the team's needs, provide guidance and support when needed, while also empower team members to take ownership of their work.

During the ideation and design phases, a collaborative and facilitative approach helps a free flow of ideas and innovation. What I've found effective is acting as more of a coach during these stages, guiding brainstorming sessions by asking thought-provoking questions and creating an environment where every contribution is valued. This approach sparks creativity and builds team confidence in the vision.

As the project goes into development, you may use a directive approach to meet deadlines by setting clear objectives, giving the team the necessary resources, and then trusting them to deliver while keeping an eye on progress. It's important to stay hands-off to empower the team, but also to make sure they're on track toward the objectives and stepping in when necessary to provide support. This balance helps maintain both accountability and progress.

A supportive leadership style would work better as deadlines approach and pressure increases, helping to boost morale and address team well-being. During high-pressure times, I've seen that acknowledging hard work and offering encouragement can go a long way in maintaining productivity and keeping the team motivated. You should recognize the human element in the process and make sure the team feels supported, not just driven.

Balancing directive and supportive leadership when tight deadlines approach is important and not an easy task. From one side you should set clear goals and make sure the team stays on track, and from the other side, support the team emotionally and psychologically.

Keep an open communication, be available to address concerns, and show appreciation for the team's efforts, to create an environment where team members feel both guided and valued.

Balancing Market Needs with Tech and Business Goals

Navigating the interaction between market demands, technology, and business objectives is a delicate balancing act that helps develop products that are technologically feasible but also meet market needs and align with the company's goals.

Understanding Market Demands

The first step to achieve this balance is to get a deep understanding of the market demands which includes market research, user feedback, and competitive analysis to identify the unmet needs, preferences, pain points and the addressable market size of your audience. Product managers must be capable of translating these insights into product features that address specific user problems, ensuring that the product meets and exceeds market expectations.

Market research must be done continuously if you want to be on top of market demands. PMs should analyze market trends and identify user needs by using surveys, interviews, focus groups, and market segmentation analysis. The data collected helps create user personas and journey maps that guide the development of product features tailored to meet the user problems and verify if the effort is worth the addressable market size.

Competitive analysis also plays an important role in understanding the market demands. By assessing the strengths and weaknesses of competing products, product managers can identify gaps in the market, inform product development and also shape marketing strategies to capitalize on competitors' gaps.

When you go through this process, think if the newly identified problems also align with the company's competitive edge. For example, if a company excels in solving cross-border money movement problems, it should prioritize opportunities in this domain over unrelated areas like mortgages or loans, even if those areas present significant market opportunities so that the company continues to leverage its strengths while gradually expanding its capabilities over time.

However, this doesn't mean avoiding new spaces entirely. Companies like Google and Amazon have succeeded in expanding into new problem domains after mastering their core businesses and becoming leaders in those areas. The key is to build a strong foundation first—becoming exceptional at solving your current customers' problems—before venturing into unrelated domains.

Leveraging Tech

With improvements in technology, product managers have a plethora of tools and platforms at their disposal to innovate their product offerings. However, the challenge is in selecting technologies that are also viable in the long term.

PMs should collaborate with the tech team to assess the feasibility of integrating new technologies into the product and understand the technical requirements, challenges, and the implications of adopting a new technology. They must balance the desire for innovation with the practicalities of development timelines, costs, and existing technical architecture.

Once a PM has evaluated the feasibility of the new technology, they can resort to prototyping and testing to evaluate how the new tech can improve the product. In this way, teams can conduct user testing to collect feedback on the functionality and usability of these innovations.

Aligning with Business Objectives

Every product initiative must align with the broader business objectives of the company including considerations of profitability, brand positioning, and market expansion goals. Product managers play an important role in ensuring that the product strategy supports these objectives, making tough decisions on prioritization, resource allocation, and timelines to maximize the business outcomes.

To achieve this, you will need a clear understanding of the company's objectives. Product managers must work closely with the leadership team to both grasp and help shape the broader business goals, whether they involve expanding into new markets, increasing market share, improving customer satisfaction, or driving innovation and to inform the product strategy, guiding the decisions on priorities, target markets, and features.

To measure how well the product supports business objectives, you will need to define specific, measurable goals for the product, such as user acquisition targets, revenue milestones, or customer satisfaction scores. In this way, product managers can track progress and make decisions to steer the product in the right direction.

Encouraging a User-Centric Product Strategy

In product, placing the user needs at the forefront of every product decision is the most important thing a PM can do. This philosophy helps create products that exceed user expectations, driving satisfaction, loyalty, and ultimately, success in the market.

Deep Dive into User Research

A user-centric product strategy begins with user research, and PMs and research teams can use a mix of qualitative and quantitative methods—such as interviews, surveys, usability tests, and analytics—to collect insights about the users' behaviors to build a rich, empathetic understanding of the users that goes beyond surface-level assumptions.

These methods allow for questions that can uncover areas of interest or concern and provide qualitative data that adds depth to the understanding of user motivations:

- Ethnographic research offers a lens into the users' natural environment, showing how they interact with the product in real-life scenarios and uncovers insights that users themselves might not be aware of, surfacing unarticulated needs and behaviors that can inform new product features.

- User testing sessions, where participants interact with prototypes or existing products, are useful to observe real-time reactions allowing product teams to iterate on designs before finalizing them.

- Analytics and usage data complement the qualitative methods by providing quantitative insights into how users use the product. Analysis of this data shows patterns and trends in usage and identifies popular features, potential pain points, and areas for improvement.

After both qualitative and quantitative data is collected, product managers must transform the data into actionable intelligence that can guide the product development process. In my experience, this transformation is where the real work begins—turning raw insights into strategic decisions that shape the product's future.

Empathy and Persona Development

Creating user personas and journey maps based on research findings helps in visualizing the user experience and enables product decisions to be grounded in a deep understanding of the user. When personas are deeply rooted in real data, they become truly powerful tools for aligning the team around a shared vision of who we're building for. These personas should include demographic details, user goals, pain points, and behavioral patterns while empathy maps can highlight what users think, feel, see, and do.

Through qualitative research methods such as interviews and ethnographic studies, product managers can build empathy and uncover the emotional and psychological drivers behind user behaviors, getting insights into what users value, fear, and aspire to achieve with the product.

Building on this foundation of empathy, persona development translates these insights into concrete, relatable character profiles that represent user segments. These profiles are narrative-driven representations that bring the user to life, making it easier for product teams to visualize their needs and design solutions that resonate on a personal level.

Personas should be integrated into the development process and product teams use personas to inform feature prioritization, design decisions, and user experience so that every aspect of the product aligns with the needs and expectations of its intended users. I've seen firsthand how effective personas can be when they're consistently referred to throughout the product development process, keeping the user's needs front and center. Personas serve as a common language across the team, as they help align designers, analysts, developers, marketers, and stakeholders around a shared understanding of the user.

Iterative Design Process

Prototyping and usability testing provide insights into how real users interact with the product and make sure design decisions are validated with users at every step, minimizing assumptions and reducing risk.

PMs and designers should create simplified versions of a product or feature to test specific hypotheses about user behavior. Prototypes can vary in fidelity, from low-fidelity sketches that outline basic concepts to high-fidelity models that closely mimic the final product and by testing these prototypes with actual users, teams can find issues with the user experience.

Once you tested the prototype, you should analyze the data collected to identify the problems and then understand the underlying reasons behind user behaviors. The insights collected from this analysis inform subsequent iterations of the design, with each cycle aiming to improve from the previous version.

The point of these iterations is to avoid committing to a single, final design from the outset which allows teams to adapt and evolve their designs based on real-world user feedback. It also promotes a culture of experimentation within product teams and by embracing the possibility of failure as a learning opportunity, teams can explore design solutions without the pressure of getting it right on the first try.

Feedback Mechanisms

Feedback mechanisms vary widely but typically include direct user research methods such as surveys, interviews, and usability testing. Surveys can be used to collect user feedback at scale and offer both quantitative and qualitative data on potential areas for improvement. Usability testing, on the other hand, provides a more focused way for observing users as they interact with the product, identifying usability issues, and exploring user behaviors in a controlled environment.

Social media and online forums are another way to collect feedback. By monitoring discussions about the product on these platforms, product teams can get insights into user sentiment, find out common questions or concerns, and identify advocates and detractors.

Acting on this feedback is what closes the loop, turning the insights into product improvements as PMs should implement changes based on user feedback, then measuring the impact of those changes on user satisfaction and product performance. One thing I've learned is the importance of communicating back to users about how their feedback has been addressed as it reinforces the value of user input and fosters a stronger relationship between users and the product.

Prioritizing Accessibility and Inclusivity

Being user centric also means ensuring that products are accessible and inclusive, serving all needs and abilities. Teams should design for accessibility from the outset and consider factors such as visual impairments, motor skills, and cognitive differences, to create products that are usable by as wide an audience as possible.

Design choices, from color contrast and font sizes to navigation structures and interactive elements, should be informed by the accessibility guidelines like the Web Content Accessibility Guidelines (WCAG) which provide a framework for creating digital content that's accessible to people with disabilities, including visual, auditory, physical, speech, cognitive, language, learning, and neurological disabilities.

Inclusivity also involves creating content and interfaces that are culturally sensitive and free from bias, so that all users feel represented, and might involve language options, imagery, and considering cultural norms in content creation. To do this effectively, teams can engage with diverse user groups with a range of abilities and backgrounds, and gain the right insights into the ways people interact with the product.

The tech implementation also plays a significant role in making products accessible and inclusive by developing with semantic HTML, keyboard navigability, alternative text for images, and implementing ARIA (Accessible Rich Internet Applications) roles where necessary. Additionally, you should adopt responsive design so that the product is accessible across a wide range of devices and screen sizes, and accommodate users in different contexts.

Measuring User Satisfaction

To understand the effectiveness of a user-centric product, it's important to measure user satisfaction through metrics such as the Net Promoter Score (NPS), Customer Satisfaction Score (CSAT), and usage statistics. These metrics provide quantitative data on how well the product meets the user needs. Additionally, defining success metrics like task success rates, user adoption, and feature adoption helps understand if users can effectively achieve their goals with the product. Retention and churn metrics also provide great insights, as they reflect how well users' expectations are being met over time—high retention indicates satisfaction, while high churn suggests potential issues that need addressing. We will cover metrics and KPIs in more depth in Chapter 4.

Customer support provides another lens through which to measure user satisfaction. PMs can analyze the nature and frequency of support contacts, as well as feedback received through support channels. Also, as we mentioned earlier, social media and online reviews can help understand the user sentiment and can reveal both positive and negative perceptions.

Embracing Adaptability

Adaptability starts with creating a mindset of openness and flexibility within the product team to enable teams to approach unforeseen challenges with creativity and resilience, rather than resistance. Let's take a look at techniques and templates to help adapt to any situation.

Scenario Planning

Scenario planning is a method that prepares product managers and their teams for future uncertainties by exploring different possible outcomes and their impacts on the product.

The process identifies key drivers of change that could affect the product or market like emerging technologies, regulatory changes, shifts in consumer preferences, or new competitors entering the market and, by examining these factors, teams can develop a range of plausible scenarios that represent different futures.

For each scenario, product teams then assess the potential challenges and opportunities the product might face.

This involves asking questions like

- How would user needs change in this scenario?

- What would be the impact on the product's value proposition?

- How could the competitive landscape change?

- What are the key risks and opportunities?

- How well-prepared are we to adapt to these changes?

- What assumptions are we making, and how might they evolve?

- What indicators should we monitor to identify which scenario is unfolding?

This analysis helps identify actions that could be taken to mitigate risks or capitalize on opportunities presented by each scenario.

Scenario planning pushes teams to think beyond the most likely or optimistic outcomes and consider a broader spectrum of possibilities, including less probable but potentially high-impact events and can help shape the product roadmap, guide investment decisions and prioritize features. It also prepares teams to act quickly and confidently when changes occur, reducing the time needed to adjust strategies in response to new information.

Pivoting Product Features

Meeting market demands, capitalizing on new opportunities, or addressing challenges sometimes requires significantly changing one or more aspects of your product—or even shifting your target audience and market focus.

A pivot may come out from insights or circumstances, such as user feedback that highlights a previously unrecognized need, changes in market trends that open new ways for differentiation, or tech advancements that offer new ways to solve user problems. Pivots may also target a new customer persona or shift to a different market entirely, especially when an emerging opportunity aligns better with the company's capabilities or goals. Regardless of the catalyst, the decision to pivot requires an evaluation of the current product strategy to ensure that the pivot aligns with the business goals and user needs.

The process of pivoting product features typically involves several steps:

1. Recognize that the current product strategy is not achieving the desired outcomes in terms of user engagement, market share, or revenue growth. It may be triggered by direct user feedback, competitive pressures, regulatory changes, or internal performance metrics.

2. Once the need for a pivot is acknowledged, product teams engage in market research, user feedback, and brainstorming sessions to explore new directions for the product features or to consider targeting a new user persona or market segment. This phase generates ideas that can transform the product's value proposition or open up new markets.

3. Before fully committing to a pivot, you should validate the new product or market direction with actual users by creating prototypes of the pivoted features and conducting user testing sessions to collect feedback on the new concept's viability.

4. With positive validation, the team moves forward with implementing the pivot. This stage requires planning across functions so that the changes are executed smoothly, with minimal disruption to existing users. If the pivot involves a market shift, marketing and sales strategies will also need to be adapted accordingly.

5. After the pivot is launched, monitor its impact on user engagement and business metrics. Based on these insights, you may need to refine the new features or market approach to fully realize their potential.

Let's now take a look at two templates that can help PMs manage significant changes:

- Change management plan template

- Stakeholder update template

Change Management Plan

A change management plan guides product managers and their teams through the process of implementing big changes within a project or organization and serves as a roadmap for navigating transitions, so that changes are effectively integrated into existing processes, without disruption to the workflow and with maximum buy-in from all stakeholders involved.

- Define the objective of the proposed change, including the specific goals and the scope of its impact. This section outlines what the change entails, which aspects of the product or process it affects, and the reasons behind the change.

- List internal and external stakeholders, their roles, and how the change impacts them as understanding stakeholder perspectives can help address concerns and boost support for the change.

- Add a communication plan that outlines how information about the change will be shared with the stakeholders, including the channels, frequency, and content of communications. It should also specify who will be responsible for delivering these communications.

- Create training and support materials as significant changes may require stakeholders to learn new skills or adapt to new processes. This part of the template explains any necessary training sessions, support resources, or documentation that will be provided to facilitate the transition.

- Add the timeline for the implementation of the change to help in planning and coordination, including milestones, deadlines, and the sequencing of activities required to execute the change.

- Assess the likelihood and impact of risks and outline strategies to address them, so that the change process is resilient.

- Include criteria for monitoring progress and evaluating the outcomes like KPIs, feedback mechanisms, and review points to understand the effectiveness of the change.

Stakeholder Update

A well-structured stakeholder update typically includes several key sections:

- A brief description of the project, its objectives, and its current status which sets the context for the update, reminding stakeholders of the project's purpose and scope.

- Highlights of milestones reached, objectives achieved, or progress made since the last update to help demonstrate forward momentum and celebrate successes.

- An overview of the next set of goals, including timelines for reaching these milestones to keep stakeholders informed about what to anticipate in the near future.

- An honest assessment of any challenges found or anticipated risks that could impact the project.

- Details of any significant changes to the project scope, timelines, or resources since the last update. This section should explain the rationale for the changes and their expected impact on the project.

- A summary of action items or next steps from the update, including any specific responsibilities assigned to stakeholders or team members.

- Contact details for the project manager or key team members for questions or discussions.

CASE STUDY: FITTRACK

Throughout the book, you will find several case studies that help you better frame the techniques covered in each chapter. These case studies have been created to showcase practical examples of these product techniques.

The company, FitTrack, has established a solid user base with its fitness tracking app, which offers features like activity logging, workout suggestions, and health monitoring. As part of their planning, the FitTrack team decided to employ scenario planning to prepare for the next three to five years.

Step 1: Identify Key Drivers of Change

The team identified two major drivers that could significantly impact their market either positively or negatively:

- New tech in wearable devices

- Changes in consumer attitudes toward health and privacy

Step 2: Develop Scenarios

Based on these drivers, the team developed four scenarios:

- Wearable technology becomes highly advanced and integrates with health apps, offering users real-time health data and personalized insights.

- Growing concerns over data privacy lead to stringent regulations on health data, making it harder for apps to collect and use health information.

- A surge in health consciousness makes fitness tracking extremely popular, with users demanding more health features.

- Users prefer DIY fitness methods and are less reliant on apps and wearables, favoring basic tools and self-researched health information.

Step 3: Assess Challenges and Opportunities

For each scenario, the team assessed how FitTrack could be affected and identified possible responses:

- Invest in R&D so that FitTrack remains compatible with the latest wearables, with real-time data and personalized health insights.

- Prioritize data security and privacy, develop features that provide users with control over their data and maintain compliance with new regulations.

- Expand FitTrack's features to include more health monitoring tools, partnerships with health professionals, and educational content on wellness.

- Diversify FitTrack's offerings to include DIY fitness challenges, community forums for sharing tips, and resources for self-guided health improvement.

Step 4: Implement and Monitor

The team decided to prioritize the investments in data privacy and security immediately, given the realistic threat of privacy pushback. Simultaneously, they began exploring partnerships with wearable manufacturers to prepare for the tech integrations. They also planned to monitor health trends and privacy regulation developments closely, ready to pivot their strategy as needed.

CHAPTER 2

Strategy Development

As we go deeper into the product universe, we're coming upon a critical step—the development of a product strategy. At its core, the product strategy is about choices. It's about deciding which opportunities to explore, which to bypass, and which to keep on the radar for future work. It's about understanding market demands, competitor moves, and user behaviors.

In this chapter, we'll dissect the layers of strategy development, from the importance of an inspiring vision to the specifics of market analysis, from understanding the very souls of our users to ensuring you stand out from the competition.

Here's what we will cover in this chapter:

1. **Creating a Vision and Strategy:** Develop a vision and strategy that aligns your team's efforts and drives your product toward long-term success.

2. **Setting Goals for Your Product:** Establish clear and actionable objectives that will direct your product decisions and keep your team focused on what truly matters.

3. **Market Analysis and Segmentation:** Gain deep insights into the market you're entering and identify opportunities and segment your audience to tailor your product's approach for maximum impact.

© Michele Galli 2025
M. Galli, *Navigating the Product Galaxy*, https://doi.org/10.1007/979-8-8688-1148-7_2

4. **Product Position and Branding:** Define your product's identity in the market and shape how your audience perceives your product by creating a strong, memorable brand that resonates.

5. **Your Product's Unique Selling Proposition:** Discover what sets your product apart and pinpoint the unique features and benefits that make your product stand out from the competition.

6. **Monetization and Revenue Strategy:** Strategize how your product will generate revenue. Plan and optimize your monetization model to ensure sustainable growth.

7. **Product Roadmapping:** Map out the key milestones that will guide your product's journey from concept to launch and beyond.

Creating a Vision and Strategy

A vision without a strategy is just a dream. A strategy without a vision is just routine work. But when vision and strategy come together, they create the path to success.

Think of every iconic product out there. The iPhone didn't just happen and Spotify wasn't because of luck. They began as visions, as dreams in someone's mind. Those dreams then transformed into strategies, which further refined into action plans.

The Vision Statement

A vision statement is the north star for your product. While it's meant to be aspirational, it's important to ensure it's grounded in reality. A vision should be a mix of understanding the market, your users' desires, and your company's strengths. Over the years, I've learned that it's easy to get caught up in overly ambitious visions that aren't rooted in what's actually achievable or even worse a vision that doesn't help the overall company's mission. My advice is to always balance aspiration with a clear understanding of what's possible and what really matters.

Imagine the long-term journey of your product and think of the impact it might have in 5, 10, or even 15 years. How it can change lives and maybe even parts of the world. A good vision should be durable, able to guide the team over at least a year. If it isn't, it may be too specific or not ambitious enough, and might need adjustments.

Your vision should be full of optimism; instead of just fixing problems, aim to highlight the possibilities, as words are powerful. For example, instead of *"Eliminating digital illiteracy,"* go for *"Empowering everyone with digital expertise."* One mistake I've seen is focusing too much on the problems in the vision statement, which can make the vision seem negative or limiting. A positive, opportunity-focused vision inspires and energizes your team and stakeholders. A strong vision paints a vivid picture of the future, one that anyone can easily understand and get excited about.

After creating your vision, share it and get feedback. Sometimes, a fresh set of eyes can add just the right touch to make your vision shine. In my experience, getting feedback early can prevent costly revisions later on, and it helps ensure that your vision resonates with a wider audience.

Most importantly, make sure that your product vision aligns with the company's vision set by the CEO and the rest of the leadership team. I've learned that alignment here is very important—not just to avoid conflicts, but to make sure everyone is moving in the same direction with shared goals.

How to Get Started with Your Product's Vision

Reverse Problem-Solving

Start by identifying the current problems, limitations, or pain points of your product. Have your team list these issues in detail. Then, work backwards to envision a future where these problems no longer exist and ask yourself and your team what changes would need to happen to eliminate these challenges. This approach helps you build a vision focused on overcoming existing barriers and creating a product that excels where it currently struggles. It has been a go-to for me because it grounds you and your team to solve problems that matter and that are blocking your company from achieving hyper-growth.

The "Why" Ladder

Ask "why?" five times in succession to go deeper into the core purpose of your product. Each answer should lead you further down the rabbit hole, helping you find the true essence of your product's existence.

I've found that this method is particularly effective when you're stuck at a crossroads—it forces you to get to the root of what really matters.

Vision Mad Libs

Use a fill-in-the-blank approach (see Table 2-1), for example: "*In* [X years], *we envision a world where* [specific outcome] *because* [reason/cause]."

Table 2-1. *Vision templates*

Template 1	"[Product/Company] *envisions a world where* [specific outcome], *empowering* [specific group] *to* [specific action]."
Template 2	*"Our dream is a* [specific landscape] *where* [specific action/outcome], *driven by* [product's key feature/quality]."
Template 3	*"By* [X year], [Product/Company] *aims to* [specific transformation], *making* [specific benefit] *accessible to all."*

The Mission Statement

When it comes to the mission statement, it's the day-to-day nature of what you're aiming to achieve, aligning your product's direction and purpose. Think of it as the route you've planned on your GPS, guiding you to the end destination—your vision.

Start by asking yourself, "What do we do every single day that gets us closer to our vision?" Is it creating a great user experience? Is it innovating constantly? Or is it building connections within a community?

Your mission should include the core functionalities and values of your product. While the vision paints a picture of the future, the mission gives direction and color to your daily activities.

A powerful way to frame the mission is by pinpointing the essence of your product. If a single word were to capture your product's soul, what would it be? For a social networking app, maybe it's "connectivity." Go deeper into that essence. If connectivity is the heart, how does your app ensure it beats? Perhaps, it's by creating digital spaces where interactions are as warm as sharing a cup of tea in person.

During this process, however, it's tempting to clog your mission statement with buzzwords, but authenticity is what makes your mission statement effective.

If you ever find yourself blocked in indecision, use the 5-whys method and ask yourself why your product exists. Then ask "why" again to your answer, and repeat until you've asked "why" five times. This process helps you drill down to the very core of your product's existence and can illuminate your mission. See, for example, Table 2-2.

Table 2-2. *Five whys*

Why are we building this fitness app?	To help people exercise.
Why?	To improve their health.
Why?	So they can live longer and feel better.
Why?	Because everyone deserves to enjoy a quality life.
Why?	Because life's moments are precious and should be maximized.

From this, a mission might emerge: "Maximizing life's moments by encouraging better health through exercise."

Template for a Mission Statement

"*We* [what your product does] *by* [how it does it] *to* [benefit for users/customers]."

Remember, while a vision is your "why," the mission is your "how" and both should work in harmony.

Strategies and Tactics

Think of strategies as the broad themes of your narrative as they set the direction and tone for your product. Strategies are informed directly by your vision and mission.

To create your strategy, imagine narrating a story. Begin by thinking of the ending—where your vision sets the scene. So, if your vision is to *"Empower every artist to monetize their art,"* your strategy might involve creating an online marketplace, collaborating with galleries, or offering digital workshops. A good strategy is like a brief, memorable story, so short and clear that you could even write it on a napkin: *"Work with top online art sites"* or *"Open an impressive shop for artists."*

Once you have these big ideas in place, it's time to go deeper with tactics. Think of tactics as the step-by-step actions for your strategies.

Tactic Template

"To support our strategy of [Big Idea], *we'll do* [specific action] *targeting* [specific group of people] *by* [a certain date].*"*

For example:

"To back our plan of joining hands with online art platforms, we will connect with sites like DeviantArt by the end of the year."

A helpful exercise is to put potential tactics on sticky notes and as you place them and shuffle around, you'll begin to identify what's urgent, what aligns well, and what might need reconsideration.

But remember, while your vision and mission serve as guiding stars, strategies and tactics should have some flexibility, as getting feedback and staying informed will often lead to changes in your approach. The end goal is to have strategies that provide direction and tactics that fuel your forward motion, giving shape to your product's journey.

Setting Goals and Targets

Your goals should be in sync with your vision, mission, and strategy.

Start with your vision. Every aspect of that vision can create several goals. For example, if your vision is to "Empower every artist to monetize their art," a goal could be, "Enable 1000 artists to make their first sale on our platform in the next year."

Then ground yourself with your mission. While your vision is your dream, your mission is your day-to-day reality, it's what you're doing now to reach that vision. Reflect on your mission's key elements. Suppose it's "offering artists the most intuitive tools to showcase their art." In that case, a possible goal might be, "Introduce three new tool features based on user feedback in the next quarter". See Table 2-3 for a template you can use.

Table 2-3. *Goals template*

Template	Example
"[Action] + [Specific feature/tool or improvement] + [Tangible benefit or result]."	"*Develop a drag-and-drop tool feature, so that artists can set up their portfolio in under 10 minutes.*"

Metrics/KPIs

Metrics and KPIs are the scoreboard of your product's journey and they give you clarity on where you stand concerning your goals.

Now, before diving into the numbers, pause to think. Why are you measuring? If you're all about changing online education and are focusing on interactive lessons, it makes sense to see how many students are completing your courses. It tells you if they find them engaging. So, the "why" leads you to the "what"—in this case, the "Course Completion Rate."

It's also about perspective, a goal like reaching one million users sounds impressive, but the depth lies in understanding the "why" behind this number. If building a big community is the goal, explore metrics like "Active Community Discussions" or "User Posts," alongside "New Sign-Ups," and ensure that the numbers you track add meaningful value and aren't just for show.

Set metrics that are clear, pertinent, and bounded by time. For example, if "Monthly Active Users" is your metric, it should tie back to your overarching strategy, and it's crucial to keep the monitoring consistent, say, monthly. However, don't get distracted by vanity numbers as loads of website visits sounds great at a party but doesn't add much value if it doesn't lead to meaningful user actions, like registrations or sales.

To make sense of all this, try the metric matrix, sketch out four areas on paper—Relevance, Ease of Measurement, Impact, and Timeliness, and place your potential metrics within these spaces. It's a good way to visualize what truly matters against what's secondary.

The Metric Matrix

Grab a sheet of paper, divide it into quadrants, and label them as Relevance, Ease of Measurement, Impact, and Timeliness. Now, drop potential metrics into these quadrants. It'll give you a visual cue on what's essential and what's nice to have (See Table 2-4 for an example).

Table 2-4. *Metric matrix*

Quadrant	Description	Example
Relevance	This quadrant is for metrics that tie directly back to your primary goals. They hold significant weight in decision-making.	If your vision revolves around creating the most user-friendly e-commerce platform, a relevant metric might be "Average Checkout Time."
Ease of Measurement	Sometimes, the most important metrics are also the hardest to track. This quadrant is for metrics that are straightforward to measure and require minimal effort.	"Daily Active Users" is often easier to measure than something like "Customer Satisfaction Score," which might need more qualitative methods.
Impact	These metrics, when moved even slightly, can have a substantial effect on your product's success.	For a subscription-based product, "Churn Rate" (the rate at which customers leave) is an impactful metric. A small increase can signal significant issues with user satisfaction.
Timeliness	Metrics that are crucial for short-term decisions fall here. They provide quick insights and might change frequently.	If you're launching a new feature and want immediate feedback, "Feature Usage in the First Week" could be a timely metric.

Turning Thoughts into Action

Now, while it's tempting to dive straight into the end, remember the importance of taking one step at a time. Prioritize strategies that can be achieved in the short term but have a significant impact on your long-term goals, rank strategies by ease of implementation and potential impact and start with those that are easy to implement but have a high impact.

Once you've decided on a strategy, get into the details as every strategy needs actionable steps and needs to be broken down into smaller tasks. For example, if your strategy involves "improving user experience," break it down to specifics like "redesign checkout flow" or "reduce app load time."

With your plan in hand, match tasks to timelines and think about when you want to start each task and when you hope to finish. Organizers like Trello or Asana can help keep track of what's up next and what's already done, making sure everyone knows their roles.

However, all said and done, be prepared for surprises and if a certain path seems blocked, find another, it's okay to reevaluate and adjust. Collect often, reflect on what's working and what's not. After all, the journey to success is all about navigating, adjusting, and moving forward with new energy. By the end of it all, you will have a clear and actionable path to your vision.

CASE STUDY: BOOKNEST

It's late 2022, and in the middle of a coffee shop, three college buddies—Alex, Jordan, and Taylor—are discussing the declining art of reading. They dream of a digital oasis for book fans worldwide, and that dream is about to get a name: BookNest.

Vision statement:

"*To make every coffee break a gateway to a new literary universe.*" The trio believes every reader should find their bookish soulmate over a cuppa!

Mission statement:

"*Empower readers to discover, share, and dive deep into tales, one click at a time.*" The plan includes book discovery, authentic reviews, and an active community.

Goals:

- Attract 100k global active users in year 1.

- Source 10k authentic book reviews within 12 months.

- Build an active forum with at least 5,000 posts every month.

Strategies and tactics:

- Collaborate with indie authors, discover hidden gems and promote fresh voices.

  - Tactic: Host monthly indie author spotlights.

- Use AI to create a recommendation system that gets reader preferences.

  - Tactic: Develop a "Taste Twin" feature to connect users with similar tastes.

- Engage with literary influencers to increase reach and make people talk about BookNest on TikTok and Instagram.

  - Tactic: Organize bi-monthly virtual book club events with influencers.

Metrics/KPIs:

- Active users count: key growth metric for BookNest.

- Quality of reviews: A user rating system to make sure reviews resonate authenticity.

- Community engagement: Monitoring weekly post interactions and discussion thread activity.

As the vision began to crystallize, Alex led user-centric workshops, tapping into the potential user pain points, Jordan got deep into market dynamics, and Taylor worked on some tech magic, coding potential app features.

Setting Goals for Your Product

The right goals in product keep teams aligned and provide direction, whether it's launching to 10,000 users in three months or achieving a 95% customer satisfaction rate, these goals give everyone a clear line of sight.

Setting SMART Goals

When setting goals, I find it useful to apply the SMART framework, which is a classic for a reason. Let's unpack each criteria.

Specific

When setting goals, it's important to be specific, as a vague objective doesn't provide clear direction. Being precise about your goals helps everyone know exactly what they are working toward and how to achieve it. I've learned that when goals lack specificity, it can lead to confusion and wasted efforts—something I've seen happen more than once in product teams. Clear, specific goals keep everyone focused and moving in the same direction.

For example, instead of a vague "we want to improve user engagement," go into specifics. Think about turning your homepage into an interactive playground for users. Is it about adding engaging features? Or perhaps a tutorial to guide new users?

An effective strategy to solidify your goals and make them specific is to answer the 5 W's. Identify the "*What, Why, Who, Where, and When*" of your objectives:

- *What exactly are we trying to achieve?*
- *Why is this particular objective important?*
- *Who will be responsible or affected?*

- *Where will this goal be implemented?*

- *When is the estimated time frame for initial results?*

Measurable

If a goal isn't measurable, how would you know if you're moving closer to or further away from your destination? Having measurable goals keeps you informed, lets you make informed decisions, and ensures you're not flying blind. In my experience, teams often feel lost when they can't track their progress. Having clear metrics in place is like having a compass—it points you in the right direction.

Instead of saying you want to "increase user sign-ups" say "increase sign-ups by 15% in the next quarter." The latter provides a specific, measurable target for you and your team.

It's also important to know your starting point. If you want to improve user engagement for example, you need to know your current engagement levels, as this baseline will guide your efforts and help you measure progress.

Achievable

Setting goals that are too unrealistic can be self-defeating. Achievable goals strike a balance between being challenging yet within the areas of possibility given current resources, constraints, and time frames. I've seen teams set goals that were too ambitious, only to get discouraged when they couldn't meet them. That's why it is important to set goals that stretch your abilities but are still within reach.

When setting goals, you should assess the tools and resources you have on hand and consider your past achievements and failures. Looking back at earlier goals can reveal good insights: Did we overreach in the past? Were we too conservative?

Yet, while reflecting on the past can guide our next steps, it's important to make sure those steps are manageable. Imagine having a long-term goal; it might seem intimidating at first, but by dividing it into smaller, actionable tasks, it becomes less about scaling a mountain and more about navigating a path. Each mini-goal, each task, serves as a step in the larger journey.

Relevant

Goals need to be relevant, fitting into the larger scheme of organizational or project objectives. When goals resonate with the bigger picture, they hold more meaning and purpose. One mistake I've made in the past was setting goals that sounded great on paper but didn't really contribute to the broader vision. Over time, I realized that every goal needs to be connected to the larger purpose to truly drive the team forward.

To set relevant goals, align each objective with your organization's broader mission and ask yourself: does this goal drive us closer to our vision? Every piece of the puzzle must connect, building toward the complete picture. Consider also the ripple effects of your goals as they should benefit not just your immediate team but a wider circle of shareholders and end users.

Time-bound

In product, time is both a friend and a rival. With clear deadlines, you create a sense of urgency, make sure resources are used efficiently, and avoid the aimless drift into the undefined. Time-bound goals offer clarity, motivation, and a way to measure progress.

Visualize your endpoint, is it a big product launch in six months, or introducing a new feature in a couple of weeks? Once you've got that date in your mind, consider breaking larger objectives into smaller milestones. Each of these mini-goals should have its own deadline, creating a roadmap toward your main target.

While sketching out these timelines, my suggestion is to make sure you're in sync with other significant dates on the company calendar as launching a product on the same day as a major industry event could be a problem.

Allow some flexibility in your timelines for unexpected challenges, but don't stretch it so far that you lose the essence of a deadline. In my experience, having a bit of buffer time can save you from last-minute stress, but it's important not to let this buffer undermine the urgency of the deadline.

Making Goals Resonate

Goals should inspire action, ignite passion, and spur motivation. You should create a connection between these goals and the individuals trying to achieve them, so that each team member feels linked to the broader vision of the product.

Every goal comes from a need and a story, by exploring the "why" of a goal, you infuse it with purpose. You should try to go beyond surface-level explanations and highlight instead the changes and the broader impacts that result from achieving that specific goal.

To drive home the essence of a complicated goal, sometimes a touch of relatability helps as well. Use familiar comparisons or stories to clarify complex objectives and anchor every objective within the grand scheme of things by showing how even minor goals contribute to the company's vision.

As the team starts achieving the goals, celebrate the achievements, no matter how small, and provide guidance when they don't. When team members feel valued, they naturally anchor deeper into the company's missions.

SMART GOALS EXAMPLES

See Tables 2-5, 2-6, 2-7, 2-8, 2-9, 2-10.

Table 2-5. *SMART goals—Tech*

Tech Startup	
Achieve a 20% increase in monthly active users by September 30th.	
Specific	Increase monthly active users of our mobile application.
Measurable	A 20% increase in active users over the next 6 months.
Achievable	Implement a referral program and improve the in-app user experience.
Relevant	Growth in active users correlates with increased ad revenue and better brand recognition.
Time-bound	Achieve this goal by September 30th.

Table 2-6. *SMART goals—Ecommerce*

E-commerce Store	
Improve the conversion rate of shopping cart conversions by 15% over Q2.	
Specific	Improve the rate of shopping cart conversions.
Measurable	Increase conversion rates by 15%.
Achievable	Redesign the checkout process, offer free shipping, and introduce new payment methods.
Relevant	Higher conversions mean increased sales without raising advertising costs.
Time-bound	Implement changes and track results over Q2.

Table 2-7. SMART goals—Healthcare

Healthcare Clinic
Reduce the average patient waiting time by 10 minutes over the next 3 months.

Specific	Reduce patient waiting time.
Measurable	Decrease average waiting time by 10 minutes.
Achievable	Hire an additional receptionist and streamline the appointment booking system.
Relevant	Improving patient satisfaction and potentially seeing more patients daily.
Time-bound	Assess improvements over the next 3 months.

Table 2-8. SMART goals—Restaurant

Restaurant
Increase weekday lunchtime orders by 25% during the upcoming summer season.

Specific	Increase weekday lunch sales.
Measurable	Achieve a 25% growth in lunchtime orders from Monday to Friday.
Achievable	Introduce a lunchtime special menu and offer loyalty cards.
Relevant	Increasing weekday sales can balance out slower periods.
Time-bound	Launch promotions and track for the upcoming summer season.

Table 2-9. *SMART goals—Educational*

Educational Institution	
Enroll 200 new students in online courses during the next academic year's enrollment period.	
Specific	Improve student enrollment in online courses.
Measurable	200 students enrolling in online classes.
Achievable	Increase online course marketing, offer early-bird discounts, and add more course variety.
Relevant	Connects to the longer term goal of tapping into the growing trend of remote learning.
Time-bound	Set the goal for the next academic year's enrollment period.

Table 2-10. *SMART goals—Fitness*

Fitness Center	
Improve member retention by decreasing the dropout rate by 30% over the next 6 months.	
Specific	Improve member retention.
Measurable	Decrease member dropout rate by 30%.
Achievable	Offer personalized fitness plans, introduce new classes, and get feedback on potential improvements.
Relevant	Retaining members is more cost-effective than acquiring new ones.
Time-bound	Implement strategies and measure outcomes over the next 6 months.

CASE STUDY: STARBRIGHT MOBILES

Back in 2020, StarBright Mobiles, a startup company, had just launched its first mobile phone model and they wanted to be "the next big thing in the mobile world." But as dreamy as it sounds, this aspiration was vague and lacked a tangible direction.

In 2021, after a year of moderate sales and mixed user feedback, the team decided they needed a better approach to goal-setting if they were to truly shine in the mobile market.

Setting SMART Goals

The product team knew they needed to improve the customer experience and address users' frustrations. But how? After brainstorming sessions and analyzing user feedback, they narrowed it down to improving the battery life, which was a common complaint among users and they decided on increasing battery life to last a full 24 hours with average use.

StarBright had to determine what "average use" meant and after collecting data, they decided it meant 5 hours of screen-on time, 1 hour of calls, and a day's worth of standby, with at least 10% battery remaining.

They collaborated with their R&D department to check that this goal was feasible and it turned out that with some software changes and a slightly bigger battery, they could hit their target without drastically increasing production costs.

In the mobile world, features pop up all the time, but was extended battery life still relevant? Market research showed that while camera quality and storage were important, having a battery that could last all day was still in the top three demands of users, making their goal highly relevant.

The team wanted to roll out this improvement in the next model, set to launch in just ten months. With a clear timeline in place, every department had a deadline to work toward.

In terms of results, the new StarBright model saw a 60% increase in sales compared to the previous year, and customer reviews loved the battery life. Their journey showcased the importance of setting clear, relevant, and achievable goals—and the success that comes when you do.

Market Analysis and Segmentation

Before going through any product journey, it's important to understand the market, as your strategy's success is tied to your comprehension of it. The market is like a living organism, always evolving, expanding, or contracting based on several factors. You should use tools like the SWOT analysis to stay updated and to navigate market changes.

A common mistake is treating the market as one big homogenous entity. It's not. Within it are multiple segments with specific needs, preferences, and pain points, and effective segmentation can mean the difference between a product that resonates and one that falls flat, so you should always go deep into demographic, psychographic, and behavioral segmentations. My most successful product launches have been those where we took the time to deeply understand and target the specific segments.

Most importantly, understand you're not alone in this race and knowing who your competitors are, their strengths, and their weaknesses can arm you with the intelligence to outmaneuver them. Porter's Five Forces is a useful tool here as it helps highlight direct competitors, potential threats from substitutes, the bargaining power of buyers and suppliers, and the intensity of competitive rivalry.

Porter's Five Forces

Developed by Michael E. Porter, this tool analyzes the competitive environment in which a product or company operates. The forces are: competitive rivalry, supplier power, buyer power, threat of substitution, and threat of new entry.

How to use Porter's five forces:

- Analyze each force, determining if it's strong or weak in your industry.

- Based on the analysis, decide if the industry is attractive for your product or not.

For example, for a messaging app (Figure 2-1):

- Competitive rivalry: High (many strong competitors like WhatsApp, Telegram)

- Supplier power: Low (cloud services are abundant)

- Buyer power: High (many alternatives available)

- Threat of substitution: High (email, social media)

- Threat of new entry: Medium (significant development and marketing costs but possible)

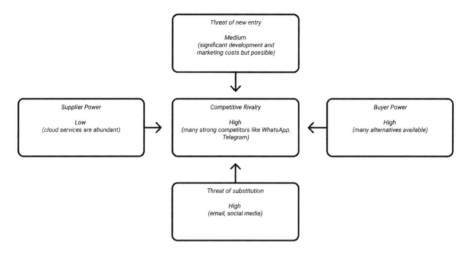

Figure 2-1. *Porter's five forces*

SWOT Analysis

The SWOT framework has stood the test of time, being equally used by a startup founder in a garage and a CEO in a high-rise.

The beauty of the SWOT analysis lies in its simplicity as it urges us to confront our product's reality in a brutally honest yet constructive way. By identifying strengths, we can amplify what works; by acknowledging weaknesses, we open up to improvements; by spotting opportunities, we align ourselves to capitalize on potential rewards; and by being aware of threats, we're better equipped to navigate challenges.

Let's break down the basics of SWOT:

- *Strengths:* These are the positive attributes that are internal to your company or product. Think of them as your superpowers, they can be tangible, like a patented technology, or intangible, like brand equity or unique company culture. Identifying these helps in creating strategies that use them to their fullest and whatever it is, if it adds value to your product or company, it's a strength.

- *Weaknesses*: No product or company is without its Achilles' heel. It might be a missing feature, a higher price point compared to competitors, or slower customer service. By identifying and understanding these vulnerabilities, strategies can be tailored to mitigate, improve, or even turn them into strengths. Be brutally honest about weaknesses as I've learned the hard way that sugar-coating issues only delays the inevitable. Addressing them head-on often leads to the most meaningful improvements.

- *Opportunities*: If strengths and weaknesses are about looking inward, opportunities are about looking outward. This quadrant represents external chances to improve your product or company's position in the market. Maybe there's a demographic segment that's underrepresented in your user base, or perhaps there's a market trend pointing toward a new feature that could be a game changer.

- *Threats*: These are external factors that could jeopardize your product's success and could range from a new competitor entering the market, regulatory changes, or a potential global economic downturn. By identifying these threats, you can prepare the right contingency plans.

Imagine you're developing a new messaging app (Figure 2-2):

- Strengths: Innovative features, strong development team

- Weaknesses: Limited marketing budget, no brand recognition

- Opportunities: Emerging markets, potential for business collaboration tools

- Threats: Established competitors, rapid technological changes

STRENGTHS	OPPORTUNITIES
Innovative features, strong development team.	Emerging markets, potential for business collaboration tools.
WEAKNESSES	THREATS
Limited marketing budget, no brand recognition	Established competitors, rapid technological changes.

Figure 2-2. *SWOT quadrants*

You can also divide it into positives/negatives and internals/externals (See Table 2-11).

Table 2-11. *SWOT example*

	Internal	External
Positive	*Strengths*	*Opportunities*
	Feature X	Emerging Market Y
	Strong Dev Team	Regulatory Change Z
Negative	*Weaknesses*	*Threats*
	Lack of Integration A	New Competitor B
	Slow Support C	Market Downturn C

Market Segmentation and Targeting

In product, you need precision targeting to avoid your product getting lost in a void of indifference. In my experience, it's hard to make a difference when we treat all customers like they are the same and an effective segmentation can 10x the impact of your features and ideas.

Let's take a look into how to segment your market to maximize your efforts.

Value Segmentation

This is based on the value that different customers represent to the company. It's a powerful technique for SaaS companies as they may segment customers into free users, monthly subscribers, and annual subscribers, each with different levels of value.

To do a proper value segmentation, you should study the user behavior and segment based on features used, time spent, and subscription levels by collecting data on the user activities and track feature usage, frequency of logins, interactions per session, and payment patterns. After that, categorize users into distinct groups. For example, in a SaaS context: "free tier users," "basic subscribers," and "premium subscribers." Then, identify patterns in each group. Maybe premium subscribers heavily use a specific set of features, while free tier users mainly use basic functionalities. Now, design upsell strategies for each segment. For example, offer feature trials to free tier users to encourage upgrades.

Needs-Based Segmentation

This is one of the segmentations I personally find most useful as it's based on the customer needs rather than the current user behaviors with your product.

Some customers might want affordability; others might want luxury. By understanding the different needs, you can create better products for them.

Start by conducting user interviews and surveys and ask questions that go deep into user desires, pain points, and expectations of your product. Once you've collected the responses, classify them into need-based categories like "affordability," "luxury," "ease-of-use," and so on and make sure your product features align with these needs.

Cultural Segmentation

This involves dividing the market on the basis of cultural origin, which is useful for global products and it allows companies to consider the cultural differences and preferences.

To do this type of segmentation, you should collaborate with cultural experts, regional teams, or locals to get insights on cultural preferences and study cultural norms, values, and preferences of the regions you are targeting. Resources like Hofstede's cultural dimensions (see Figure 2-3) can be a good starting point. At the same time, partner with local influencers or experts to get deeper insights into the cultural differences and make necessary adjustments to the product based on their feedback. It can be as simple as changing color themes for a region or as complex as adding features to accommodate specific regional needs, such as offering localized payment methods or modifying the layout to match cultural expectations of web navigation. For example, Booking.com adapts its platform significantly for regions like China and Japan, adjusting payment options, imagery, and user flow to suit local preferences.

HOFSTEDE'S CULTURAL DIMENSIONS

Developed by Geert Hofstede, a Dutch social psychologist, this theory identifies six dimensions of national culture that can help in understanding differences in behavior across countries (Figure 2-3). For product managers, particularly those working in international markets, it can be useful to understand these dimensions to tailor strategies for each unique market.

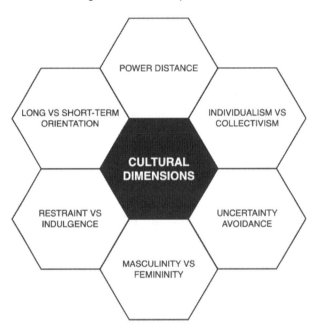

Figure 2-3. *Hofstede's cultural dimensions*

1. **Power Distance**

    It describes the extent to which less powerful members of institutions and organizations within a country expect and accept that power is distributed unequally. In high power distance countries, hierarchical structures are more accepted, and there's respect for authority and products directed at this audience might emphasize respect, tradition, or authority. On the other hand, in low power distance cultures, emphasis on equality and collaboration might resonate better.

2. **Individualism vs. Collectivism**

   This dimension focuses on the degree to which people in a society are integrated into groups. In individualistic societies, products and messaging should focus on personal success, individual achievements, and personal freedoms while in collectivist societies, the emphasis should be on community, family, and group achievements.

3. **Masculinity vs. Femininity**

   This dimension looks at the role distribution between the genders in a society. Masculinity in Hofstede's original model implies a preference for heroism, assertiveness, and material rewards, while femininity stands for a preference for cooperation, modesty, caring for the weak, and quality of life.

   Knowing whether a target audience leans toward masculine or feminine cultural values can help in creating product features and marketing narratives. In today's modern society we try to break away from stereotypes, you should nonetheless be aware where each audience stands.

4. **Uncertainty Avoidance**

   This dimension relates to the extent to which people feel threatened by uncertainty and the unknown, and try to avoid these situations. In high uncertainty avoidance cultures, guarantees, clear instructions, and a sense of security might be essential in product offerings, while in low uncertainty cultures, taking risks or trying new innovative features might be more acceptable.

5. **Long-Term Orientation vs. Short-Term Orientation**

   This dimension looks at how societies value long-term commitments and respect for tradition. In a long-term oriented culture, products that emphasize durability, legacy, and long-term benefits might resonate better. In short-term oriented cultures, people might prefer immediacy, quick results, and current trends.

6. **Indulgence vs. Restraint**

   This dimension is about the extent to which members in a society try to control their desires and impulses. In indulgent societies, marketing might focus on self-gratification, enjoying life, and having fun. In restrained societies, the emphasis might be on discipline, order, and resisting temptations.

Competitive Analysis

Product managers need a clear understanding of the market's competitive landscape. Competitive analysis is the process by which a company evaluates its competitors' strengths and weaknesses and can help identify what makes its product unique, as well as discover potential opportunities.

When you do a competitive analysis, it's important you understand the why behind what you see as it's easy to see a feature and think, "we need that!" But understanding why a competitor has chosen a certain path is a better way.

For example, if a competitor is offering a free feature that you charge for, rather than immediately making your feature free, investigate. Are they monetizing elsewhere? Is this a loss leader for a bigger product suite? Going into the "why" can prevent knee-jerk reactions that might not serve your product in the long run.

Competitive analysis also covers brand perception, marketing strategies, customer sentiment, and even company culture, as sometimes a brand's strength isn't just its product features but its customer service or its community.

Let's take a look at some useful techniques for your competitive analysis.

Feature Comparison Matrix

A straightforward grid that lists out features on one axis and competitors on the other, allowing for a direct comparison. Beyond listing features, this matrix can also include user feedback on each feature, pricing, and even technical robustness.

How to use it:

- Create a table with your product and competitors' in the top row.

- List down all possible features or service points in the columns.

- Mark which product has which feature, or rate them on a scale (e.g., 1–5).

- Analyze gaps and overlaps.

Always consider the importance of each feature—having more doesn't always mean better; the key is having the right features that resonate with your target users.

Pricing Strategy Analysis

As part of your market research, you should understand how your pricing stands relative to competitors, and determine if it provides the right perceived value. Subscription models, freemium offerings, one-off pricing—each of these tells a story about target markets, business goals, and perceived product value.

How to use it:

- Document the pricing strategies of all competitors.

- Consider the value proposition for each. Is a higher price justified by more features or better quality?

- Assess your own pricing. Are you undercharging? Overcharging? Is there an opportunity for a freemium model?

Remember, price perception plays a big role. Apple products, for example, are premium-priced, but many consumers are willing to pay due to the perceived value.

CASE STUDY: PLANETARYTECH

Founded in 2021, PlanetaryTech aimed to revolutionize urban planning with eco-friendly solutions and they developed an AI-driven software that could optimize city plans for green spaces and sustainable housing. But entering the market was a challenge with dominant players like UrbanEco and CityGreen and their objective was to secure a 10% market share within two years.

SWOT analysis:

- Strengths: Cutting-edge AI-driven algorithms; a passionate team with expertise in both tech and environmental science.

- Weaknesses: Limited brand recognition; initial funding running out.

- Opportunities: Emerging markets in Asia and Africa; cities aiming for "Green" status.

- Threats: Dominant competitors; rapid technological changes could render their current algorithms outdated.

Porter's five forces:

- Rivalry among existing competitors: High. Dominated by UrbanEco and CityGreen.

- Threat of new entrants: Moderate. AI-driven solutions were trending, but barriers like domain expertise and initial investment were significant.

- Bargaining power of buyers: High. Cities and governments had ample options.

- Bargaining power of suppliers: Low. Most tech solutions were open-source or self-developed.

- Threat of substitutes: Low. Traditional urban planning couldn't achieve the efficiency of AI-driven solutions.

Feature comparison matrix (Table 2-12):

Table 2-12. *Feature comparison*

Feature/Competitor	PlanetaryTech	UrbanEco	CityGreen
AI-Driven Optimization	Advanced	Intermediate	Basic
Green Space Planning	Comprehensive	Basic	Advanced
Transportation Planning	Intermediate	Advanced	Intermediate
Sustainable Housing Solutions	Advanced	Basic	Intermediate
Usability and Interface	User-friendly	Technical	Moderate
Integration with Existing Systems	Seamless	Moderate	Challenging
Training and Support	Comprehensive	Limited	Comprehensive

From this matrix, PlanetaryTech identified that while UrbanEco was leading in transportation planning, and CityGreen had an edge in green space planning, neither was fully capitalizing on sustainable housing and this became PlanetaryTech's main focal point, a niche they could dominate.

Pricing analysis:

Competitor pricing:

- UrbanEco: Subscription model priced at $25,000/month for cities with a population of less than 500,000, $45,000/month for larger cities.

- CityGreen: Flat fee of $30,000/month with additional support and features available at added costs.

Recognizing the dominance of subscription models, PlanetaryTech introduced a three-tier system:

- Freemium: For towns with a population of less than 100,000. Limited features but enough to make impactful changes.

- Standard: $15,000/month for cities with a population between 100,000 to 500,000. Full suite of features but limited support.

- Premium: $25,000/month for larger cities. Includes support, training sessions, and regular feature updates.

The freemium model was introduced to gain a foothold in smaller markets. The slightly lower price points for their standard and premium plans attracted potential switchers from UrbanEco and CityGreen.

While the freemium model allowed many smaller towns to experience the benefits of PlanetaryTech, the conversion rate from freemium to standard was initially lower than expected. However, the standard and premium plans were well-received, especially when cities compared feature sets and recognized PlanetaryTech's edge in sustainable housing solutions.

Product Position and Branding

Your brand is about the story you tell, the feelings you evoke, and the space you occupy in a consumer's mind and you can think of it as the "personality" of your product. It's how your audience perceives you and why they would choose you over a myriad of other options.

Why Branding Matters

We're inundated with choices. Walk down any supermarket aisle, and you'll see ten different versions of the same product. Why do we reach for one over the other? Often, it's branding. Rather than buying a product, we're buying into a story, a feeling, a promise. Branding creates that emotional connection.

Product positioning is the art of making your product feel tailor-made for its target audience, so that it stands out in the marketplace. Without going deep into your audience's lifestyle, preferences, and habits, your product may fail. The more specific you can get about their day-to-day life, their aspirations, and their problems, the better, as this insight will make your product resonate with them, making them feel it was created just for them.

In a competitive market, your product's unique attributes are what set it apart, it's that specific feature or detail that makes a user think, "This product is just perfect for me."

Once you've identified this key element, avoid changing it too often, as it could confuse your users. Brands that leave a lasting impression are anchored in their core values, whether it's championing sustainability or driving innovation, and in a world with countless options, staying authentic and consistent will help your audience connect with you.

How to Create a Good Brand Identity

In product, the story starts with a fundamental question: "Why?" which goes deeper than revenue or market share; it touches the company's purpose, the change the product hopes to inspire and the difference it aspires to make.

So how does one uncover this "why"? You should start from within with open conversations with your team, as every individual, from the product manager to the intern, holds a piece of the brand's story. Then, engage with your brand's earliest supporters—the customers or stakeholders who believed in your vision from the beginning as their perspectives can highlight the aspirations tied to your brand so that your product positioning remains rooted in genuine user sentiment.

Define Your Brand Attributes

Creating your brand's identity is a long journey and you need to understand what emotions and responses you want to trigger. In branding, defining your unique attributes serves this purpose. For example, think whether you want your brand to be quirky or solemn, or cutting-edge versus rooted in tradition, as these choices will influence every aspect of your brand, from the font in your logo to the voice of your marketing campaigns.

Visualize a mental scale that contrasts brand attributes, such as innovative versus timeless or casual versus formal and by placing your brand along these mental scales, you can select the personality you wish to project. Once you have done that, make sure to collect feedback from your internal team and a selected audience segment and prompt them with quick adjectives they associate with your brand. These associations show the current perception and help steer your brand in the right direction.

At the same time, make sure to analyze your marketplace peers as well, but instead of viewing them only through a competitive lens, treat them as reference points and look at how they mold their brand personas and narratives as it can help you understand if your brand is in a unique space in the minds of your audience.

Decide Your Visual Elements

This is about defining the visual elements like logos, typography, and the color spectrum. These are the tangible pieces that, when combined, create your brand's personality and should echo the sentiments of your target audience as they have the power to capture the attention in the marketplace.

One approach for this is hosting design workshops and gathering people from different domains such as design, marketing, and even product management.

Another good way to find inspiration and great designs that align with your brand's vibe is to create mood boards on platforms like Pinterest.

But while your intuition and expertise hold great value, the true test of any visual lies in its reception by the audience and here you can A/B test variants of your designs with selected groups and get insights into their preferences.

Develop Your Brand Voice

In the world of branding, more important than *what* you say is *how* you say it and the cadence of your words, the emotions they trigger, and the tone they carry encapsulate the personality of your brand.

You should define them in your content guidelines and consider these guidelines as a blueprint that shapes every narrative of your brand. Imagine if your brand were to take on a distinct personality—what traits would it have? Would it be bold and daring, or steady and resilient?

Consistent Branding

Whether it's your website, social media, or even an email signature, your branding should be consistent and a brand manual can help you do that. It maps out the details—from logo placements and the shades of your colors to the typographic choices and the cadence of your brand's voice. Distribute this manual to your team so that everyone is on the same page and knows how to talk about your brand.

CASE STUDY: SOLARBRITE

SolarBrite wanted to provide solar-powered lanterns to rural communities without reliable electricity, but despite a worthy cause and a quality product, they faced a lot of competition from established brands and cheaper, low-quality imports.

Before jumping into branding activities, the SolarBrite team took a week off to the villages they wanted to serve and while interacting with the local community, they understood the need for a dependable light source that children could study under and artisans could work with. The key insight was that they weren't selling lanterns; they were selling hope and empowerment.

Feedback from the communities showed three words that kept popping up—"Dependable," "Bright," and "Long-lasting," and these became their brand attributes. They decided to position themselves as the "reliable light in the darkest nights."

For visual elements, SolarBrite wanted something that felt connected to the communities they served. The logo they designed was a radiant sun merging with a traditional lantern, symbolizing a blend of modern solar technology with the rustic, rural feel while the colors they chose were warm yellows and earthy browns, symbolizing sunlight and grounded reliability.

The voice they chose was assuring, and slightly aspirational. SolarBrite's communications always contained stories—of kids studying under the lantern, of artisans creating late into the night—and their tagline was "SolarBrite—Lighting up futures."

Every touchpoint, from product packaging to their website, had a consistent branding and the lanterns came with a small booklet, telling the brand story and explaining its commitment to lighting up lives. SolarBrite's strong positioning and branding managed to stand out in the market and their brand also became synonymous with trust and quality. The brand had built an identity that resonated with its core audience.

Your Product's Unique Selling Proposition

In a market filled with countless products competing for consumer attention, only a few truly stand out and capture people's interest, so what makes these products different? They have something unique that sets them apart, a distinct quality or feature that resonates strongly with consumers. This is where your product's unique selling proposition (USP) comes into play. The USP is what creates that "Oh, I need this!" moment for your audience, making your product memorable.

Creating a USP

Before you even think of your USP, you need to understand what's out there and understand what your competitors are missing. Google Trends, Amazon and Yelp reviews, SEMrush, or even a classic SWOT analysis can be quite helpful.

Imagine you're launching a new line of trendy sneakers (Table 2-13), Competitor A focuses on athletic performance, while Competitor B emphasizes sustainability. Now, what if your product combined both performance and eco-friendliness? That combination could make your product stand out.

Table 2-13. Competitors

Competitor	Their USP	What they lack	Opportunities
Competitor A	Performance sneakers	Not eco-friendly	Eco-friendly performance shoes
Competitor B	Sustainable materials	Less durable	Durable and sustainable shoes

Customer Feedback and Surveys

Start casual; you could chat with folks on social media or get a bit more formal with SurveyMonkey or Google Forms, but remember to ask the right questions, like, "What do you look for in a [product]?" or "Ever felt something's missing when using [products]?" By the end of this, you'll have a good idea of what people are looking for.

A template for a short survey is given in Table 2-14.

Table 2-14. Short survey

Question	Why it's important
What's the one thing you feel is missing in [current product you use]?	Find gaps
Describe your ideal [product]	Understands the user's perfect scenario

Your Unique Statement

Use all the insights you've got to draft a short yet punchy statement, keep it simple, make it memorable, and make sure it genuinely represents what you and your product stand for. Create multiple versions of your USP, then refine as the first draft is rarely perfect, but it's a start.

See, for example, a template for creating your USP in Table 2-15.

Table 2-15. *USP template*

Feature/Insight	Benefit	Potential USP Statement
Quick Brew Tech	Saves time	*"Morning joe in a flash. Coffee ready before you are!"*

Things to Keep in Mind While Creating the USP

Creating your product's USP is all about emotion and you should consider what sentiment you want to evoke in your customers. For an eco-friendly sneaker, for example, it may be an invitation into its sustainable nature: "Step into a greener future, one sneaker at a time." However, make sure the message is concise; you want your USP to stick with no need for long explanations—get straight to the point.

A powerful USP should also tackle a real problem and it should resonate with a challenge your customers face or something they value and the more precise you are with your offer the more power you have. Specific promises have this charm about them, making them irresistible, claiming "lose up to 10 pounds in a month" feels way more concrete than just "lose weight quickly."

Another good way to come up with a good USP is thinking about iconic brand slogans that just stick. Apple's "Think Different" or M&M's delightful "Melts in your mouth, not in your hand" are touches of genius. Analyze what makes them tick, how they stand out, and draw inspiration, but, of course, keep it original—no copycats!

Lastly, keep it real, as your USP should transmit authenticity. Customers have a sixth sense for sniffing out overhyped claims, so stay true, genuine, and up-front about what you offer.

CASE STUDY: GREENSTRIDE

GreenStride, a once-small startup in the world of athletic footwear, had a brilliant idea: creating shoes from ocean plastic, but faced a market dominated by big names like Nike and Adidas.

GreenStride's initial USP was, "high-quality athletic shoes made from ocean plastic." It was direct, yes, but it failed to truly impact and they got sucked in with every other eco-friendly shoe brand, and sales were modest at best.

GreenStride realized they needed a better connection, so they decided to rework their USP. They invited potential customers to workshops, conducted surveys, and held brainstorming sessions with their team and they asked questions like, "what does 'saving the ocean' mean to you?" and "describe the feeling of wearing a shoe that's both comfy and eco-friendly."

People loved the environmental angle, but they wanted more—a story, an emotion, an experience.

One evening, after a particularly intense brainstorming session, a team member voiced a memory: "I remember watching a documentary on marine life and how plastic affects them, I felt terrible and wished I could do something." That was the lightbulb moment, "GreenStride: Step into a cleaner ocean." Each shoebox was redesigned to include stories of marine life affected by ocean plastic and customers were joining a movement rather than just buying shoes, they added QR codes on the box which led to mini-documentaries on ocean conservation efforts and also launched a campaign where customers could send in their used GreenStride shoes for recycling.

Within six months, GreenStride's sales skyrocketed, they had a narrative, a cause, an identity. They collaborated with ocean conservation NGOs, sponsored beach cleanup drives, and soon found themselves featured in major magazines and talk shows.

Monetization and Revenue Strategy

Alright, it's time to talk about money! After all, it's the revenue that keeps the lights on and the servers running. Your revenue strategy is the bridge connecting great products with sustainable businesses.

To find the right revenue strategy you need to ask yourself the right questions:

- *What's my product's value?* Before asking for money, understand what unique value you bring to the table, is it convenience, a unique feature, an experience?

- *Who's my audience?* Teenagers probably won't spend $100/month, but businesses might if you save them thousands.

- *How do users interact with my product?* Is it a daily engagement or a once-in-a-while purchase?

- *Where's the sweet spot?* Price too high, and you'll scare off potential users, too low, and you might not cover costs or devalue your offering.

Learning from the Legends

Apple's ecosystem is legendary, once you're in, every addition feels like a natural next step, creating an integrated, seamless experience. Dropbox attracted users with free storage, and as their digital needs grew, the shift to a paid plan became almost inevitable. Airbnb, instead of competing directly with hotels, tapped into the experiential travel segment, enabling locals to monetize their spaces while offering travelers a more authentic experience. The common thread among these companies is their approach to monetization—they didn't impose a revenue model on their product, instead, they deeply understood their users, iterated, and developed a monetization strategy that felt organic and natural.

Finding Your Perfect Fit

Diving into monetization can be both exciting and scary and it's important to understand which model fits with your product and your audience. When considering a monetization model, you should carefully analyze your costs as well—whether they are up-front, recurring, fixed, or variable.

Freemium

The freemium model is where you offer the basic version of your product for free and then charge for the more advanced features. Spotify is a classic example, while users can listen for free, they get ad interruptions, if they want ad-free listening with some extra features, there's a fee attached. The challenge is offering enough in the free version to attract users but keeping the best bits behind the paywall.

Freemium is a powerful acquisition tool because it eliminates entry costs, pushing a larger pool of users to try out your product. This user base also acts as a source of feedback, allowing you to iterate and improve your offering. As users become accustomed to the free version and start recognizing its value, they are more likely to upgrade to paid tiers when they require advanced features. This strategy effectively converts free users into paying customers, using the initial free access to build a solid, monetizable customer base.

Freemium models work well when there is a distinct differentiation between basic and advanced features as the free version must remain usable and valuable while converting users with more sophisticated features in the paid version, designed to be used by power users or businesses. This model is particularly effective for mass-market products targeting a broad audience, like Trello or Dropbox and for products with built-in virality like social sharing or invite-based features.

When to Avoid Freemium

A freemium model might not work for niche products targeted at a specific audience as in these cases, offering too much for free might not be good, and a trial period could be better at converting users to paying customers.

You should also consider the cost of supporting a large number of free users. If the conversion rate to paid users is low, you may end up having significant expenses without a return on investment.

There's also a psychological aspect to consider; if the free version of your product is too generous, users might see little value in upgrading to the premium version, thinking, "Why pay when I'm already getting so much?" This can undermine the perceived value of your product and affect your profitability.

It's important to find the right balance with your free version—it should be good enough to attract users but not so good that they see no need to upgrade. Keep an eye on conversion rates and be ready to adjust the features offered in the free and paid tiers to optimize the upgrades. Also, make sure you clearly communicate the value in upgrading, regular prompts about what users are missing in the free tier can help them switch to the paid version, but it's important to avoid being too pushy.

Subscription

Here, users pay a periodic fee to get access to your product or service. Take Netflix, for example, subscribers pay monthly to access TV shows and movies. The complexity here comes from updating and refreshing your content or features to justify the recurring payments.

The subscription model is great for its ability to generate predictable and consistent revenue streams, which simplifies the business financial planning and forecasting, provides an immediate influx of cash at the beginning of each billing cycle, and also encourages customer loyalty as users are more likely to engage with the product regularly, improving their connection to the brand. As users become more integrated and familiar with the product, you can also introduce higher-tier plans with additional features.

Opt for a subscription model when your product delivers ongoing value, such as streaming services like Netflix or Spotify. This model is also particularly good for Software-as-a-Service products that frequently update and improve, offering users new features that justify ongoing payments. Consider both fixed and variable recurring costs to make sure the subscription price provides sufficient margin for the content updates. If you expect a high customer LTV — meaning once users are onboard, they are likely to stay for long periods — a subscription model can maximize revenue over time.

When to Avoid Subscription

Consider avoiding subscription models when your product offers value that is short-term or doesn't require regular use as this type of model might be good for users who do not perceive ongoing value. Additionally, in markets saturated with subscription services—from software to everyday consumer goods—there is a growing phenomenon of "subscription fatigue" and potential customers overwhelmed by their existing subscriptions may not want to commit to another recurring payment.

Price sensitivity can also play a significant role, if customers perceive the subscription as financially heavy over time, even if it offers better value, they may prefer a single-purchase option. This scenario often happens in highly competitive markets where consumers are careful about their spending habits and the accumulation of monthly charges.

Make sure your subscription fees are fair and in line with both the perceived and actual value of your product to avoid overpricing or underpricing. The plans should also be flexible; by offering multiple plans such as monthly, yearly, or family packs, you can satisfy different customer needs and financial situations. You should also provide easy options for users to upgrade, downgrade, or cancel their subscriptions to improve their experience and trust in your service.

One-Time Purchase

In the one-time purchase, users pay once, and they get lifetime access to the product; many software applications and video games follow this approach. It's important to ensure the product offers long-term value, making the one-time cost seem worth it.

A one-time purchase model is usually simple and convenient for customers, as it eliminates the need for them to manage recurring payments and it is a good approach for users who prefer a single transaction, giving them full access without additional costs. For businesses, this model brings an immediate revenue boost, as payments are received up-front rather than spread out over time, improving the liquidity of the business; it reduces admin work associated with managing complex billing cycles and reduces the problems of handling payment failures.

You should use a one-time purchase model when your product offers a finite value proposition, such as software licenses that expire, special reports, or premium games that don't require content updates. This model is often used by products with a clearly defined lifespan or those that provide value in a single instance, making it straightforward for customers to understand what they are paying for. The one-time purchase can attract customers who are unsure about long-term commitments; the up-front, one-time fee is perceived as less heavy than recurring payments.

Market perception also plays a role; in some sectors or for certain products, customers are used to paying once and may resist transitioning to a subscription model. In these cases, using familiar buying patterns may help with sales, as it avoids the issues associated with changing the consumer behaviors.

When to Avoid the One-Time Purchase
You should avoid the one-time purchase model when your business model requires a consistent, predictable revenue stream, as this method does not provide the recurring income that subscriptions offer. In scenarios where acquisition costs are high, the initial revenue generated from a single purchase may not be enough to cover these costs, making the financial sustainability of one-time sales questionable.

This model often results in limited engagement post-purchase as well; without the regular interaction provided by subscription renewals, you will have fewer opportunities for upselling or cross-selling and it can lead to issues in keeping a relationship with the customer, potentially impacting the long-term business growth.

When using a one-time purchase model, you should make sure that customers perceive the value of their purchase as exceeding the cost. This sense of immediate value is important for the customer's satisfaction and can be improved by offering optional paid add-ons, which provides similar benefits without requiring a subscription. Customers must also fully understand what the purchase includes and should not be left unsure about the product's features, benefits, or any potential additional costs. Bundling products or services can also increase value perception by offering them at a discounted rate.

Advertising

With the advertising model, you allow free access to your product but generate revenue by displaying ads to users, think Facebook or Instagram. The balancing act here is providing a great user experience while integrating ads effectively, so they don't become intrusive.

Advertising offers products or content to users for free, which is a major draw for growth as it lowers the barrier for entry, allowing to create a large user base quickly, which in turn makes the platform more appealing to advertisers.

Once the advertising system is in place, it can provide a passive income stream that requires little to no active management. This scalability makes the model attractive, as it continually increases the platform's value to current and potential advertisers. More users attract more advertisers, and the revenue from ads can be reinvested into improving the product, which then attracts more users.

Before adopting an advertising model, evaluate the costs involved—such as infrastructure, maintenance, and user acquisition costs—against the potential ad revenue. Since ad revenue is largely volume-based, the costs to build and maintain a large user base need attention to avoid losses.

Opt for advertising when your platform has high traffic but low likelihood of direct transactions from users. This model is good for content-heavy platforms such as blogs, news sites, and video-hosting platforms, where the primary benefit is the content itself, which naturally attracts a large audience.

The viewership is an attractive aspect for advertisers, making it a viable source of revenue, if your user base is diverse, it becomes a good target for advertisers from different sectors looking to reach different demographics. In these cases, advertising can generate substantial income by leveraging the volume and variety of your audience without requiring payments from users for access to the content.

When to Avoid Advertising

Consider avoiding advertising if it risks compromising the user experience, excessive ads can annoy users, driving them away and increasing churn rates.

Advertising revenue is highly dependent on maintaining large user volumes; if your platform experiences a drop in user numbers or struggles to attract a substantial audience, the model becomes less effective and potentially unsustainable. You should also take into consideration today's climate of data privacy concerns, where users are more wary of platforms that collect personal information to sell to advertisers.

When using the advertising model, you should prioritize the user experience above all else and make sure advertisements feel organic and do not disrupt the user's journey. Instead of relying only on traditional banner ads, diversify your approach by using video ads, native ads, and sponsored content to understand what best resonates with your audience without compromising the quality of their experience.

Data plays a key role in this model; the more detailed and accurate your user data, the more attractive your platform becomes to advertisers looking for opportunities. However, at the same time, make sure to be transparent in how the user data is used to create trust and ensure compliance with the privacy laws—a breach in this area can significantly damage your reputation and user trust.

Affiliate Marketing

Affiliate marketing is a model where you promote someone else's product on your platform, and with each sale or click generated through your link, you earn a commission. A lot of bloggers and influencers adopt this model but you should promote products that resonate with your brand and audience.

Affiliate marketing is a performance-based revenue model where you pay only for tangible results, whether it's sales or specific user actions, which make sure you maximize the return on every penny spent and extends your marketing reach by leveraging affiliates who can introduce your product to new audiences and markets that might otherwise remain untapped.

Because the costs are incurred only when actual sales happen, the financial risk associated with affiliate marketing is significantly lower compared to other marketing strategies and makes it an attractive option for businesses looking to expand their reach while maintaining control over their marketing budgets.

Affiliate marketing is used for products with a broad appeal, as it allows you to leverage affiliates to reach new market segments and expand your reach significantly. This strategy is also good in niche markets where specialized affiliates can target and influence specific consumer groups who are likely interested in your unique offerings, but it's important to partner with affiliates that have a credible reputation so that your product is represented accurately and positively. Also, when using affiliate marketing, analyze the commission payments to affiliates against expected returns to evaluate if this strategy makes financial sense.

Digital products and services, such as e-books, online courses, software subscriptions, and more, are also well-suited for affiliate marketing as these products typically have higher margins and the digital format helps the global distribution, making it a great tool for scaling reach and maximizing profits without geographical limitations.

When to Avoid Affiliate Marketing
Avoid affiliate marketing if your product operates on low margins as the commissions paid to affiliates could make sales unprofitable by narrowing the margins. It's also a risk to rely too much on affiliates for generating sales, so it's important to have a diversified marketing strategy that doesn't depend solely on one channel.

There's also a risk of brand dilution; if affiliate-programs are not managed, there's a possibility that affiliates might misrepresent your brand and cause some inconsistencies in how your brand is perceived and potentially harm your reputation in the market.

Outline the terms of engagement for your affiliates as clarity helps both you and your affiliates understand the compensation structure, expected behavior, and other important details of your partnership. It's also important to conduct regular audits of affiliate activities to ensure they comply with these terms and accurately represent your brand. Also, make sure to disclose affiliate links to customers to encourage trust, transparency, and honesty in your marketing.

Dynamic Pricing

Companies like Uber use dynamic pricing where the pricing changes in real time based on certain factors, like demand. However, you will need to be transparent and make sure customers don't feel taken advantage of.

Dynamic pricing works in cases where the demand fluctuates significantly, for example, during special events, peak holiday seasons, or periods of product scarcity, and allows businesses to capitalize on these variations by changing prices in real time.

To use this model you will need a strong data infrastructure, as it relies heavily on real-time data about customers, competitors, and market trends and by using this data, you will be able to maximize profits while maintaining competitive prices. In markets crowded with competitors, dynamic pricing can serve as a differentiator, helping your business stand out by offering prices that attract customers while protecting your margins.

Dynamic pricing is used by high-frequency purchase products like airline tickets or hotel rooms, where consumer price sensitivity is high and shoppers are continuously searching for the best deals and it is also used for perishable goods or services, like event tickets or fresh produce, which require timely sales before they expire; dynamic pricing helps in maximizing the revenue during the availability window.

Digital goods, which carry virtually no inventory costs, like e-books, online courses, or software, are also good candidates for dynamic pricing. You can dynamically adjust prices based on demand, competition, and other market factors, and optimize revenue for products where storage and distribution costs are minimal.

When to Avoid Dynamic Pricing

Avoid dynamic pricing if there is a risk of losing customer trust as consumers may feel exploited if they perceive price increases during high-demand periods as unfair. You should not underestimate the complexity of implementing dynamic pricing either as it requires sophisticated algorithms and strong data analytics capabilities which can be resource-intensive.

You should then take into consideration the legal and ethical concerns, as in some regions or industries, regulations may prohibit some forms of dynamic pricing, particularly those that could be interpreted as price gouging. Be open and transparent about why prices change to help customers understand and accept these changes, reducing the likelihood of them feeling taken advantage of and although it may be tempting to maximize the profits during peak demand, consider a price cap to avoid losing customers because of excessively high prices.

CASE STUDY: STELLARSPACE

StellarSpace is a platform that offers an immersive virtual space exploration experience where users can travel through galaxies, visit planets, and even create their own stars.

Being new in the market, StellarSpace had little idea about how users would respond to different monetization models and the initial user feedback showed great interest, but converting that interest into revenue was a big unknown.

StellarSpace initially went with a one-time purchase model and set the price at $49.99. However, potential users didn't want to spend $49.99 up-front for something they hadn't tried. Also, the one-time purchase left no room for recurrent revenue, and the team realized that they needed funds for the updates and maintenance.

After analyzing the user feedback and by taking inspiration from other successful platforms, the team introduced a freemium model where users could explore a limited part of the universe for free while specific galaxies, exclusive content, and stars creation tools became premium features which allowed users to get a taste before committing.

The team also recognized the diversity of their audience and introduced three subscription tiers:

- $5.99/month: Basic exploration with some premium galaxies.

- $9.99/month: More galaxies, and basic stars creation tools.

- $14.99/month: Full access, including advanced stars creation tools.

After seeing a significant interest from multiple global regions, they adjusted the prices based on the regional purchasing power which led to a spike in subscriptions from Asia and South America.

Finally, the team used special events like meteor showers or black hole discoveries as occasions for limited-time discounts or bonus features.

The shift to a freemium + subscription model led to a steady flow of revenue, allowing the team to keep working on updates and improvements as the localized pricing opened up new user demographics, and the seasonal promotions increased user engagement significantly.

Product Roadmapping

Every product is a universe in its own right, but the universe wasn't built overnight. It took time and a precise sequence of events to evolve through chaos. Similarly, your product won't magically find its trajectory without that sequence of events, your roadmap.

The MVP

No product starts off perfect and the key to early success is to avoid overcomplicating your product from the beginning. Focus on identifying and refining your Minimum Viable Product—the essential features that solve your users' primary problem.

Starting simple doesn't mean limiting your product's potential; it means building a strong, user-centric foundation where, instead of trying to include every idea from the start, you concentrate on creating a product that is clear, intuitive, and easy to use, ensuring that your product's core purpose remains strong and resonates with users. As your product gains traction, you can gradually introduce additional features, but only if they add real value without complicating the user experience. By beginning with a solid MVP, you set your product up for long-term growth and success.

Feature Prioritization: What Makes the Cut?

During feature prioritization you've got countless ideas, but only the most valuable should make it to the roadmap.

The RICE scoring method is quite useful for evaluating the reach, impact, confidence, and effort of each feature, but before prioritizing any feature, take a moment to reflect on its purpose and impact. If the underlying purpose isn't clear and the impact is not there, it might be best to leave it out. You should then assess the costs and effort of the feature; costs include the development time, complexities, and potential deviation from the main plot.

Another commonly used prioritization method is MoSCoW:

- Must have: Non-negotiable. The product can't function without it.

- Should have: Important but not critical. You'd want it in the next iteration.

- Could have: Nice to have if time or resources allow.

- Won't have (*this time*): Deprioritized, not for the current cycle.

Get your team together, discuss each feature, and categorize them in the MoSCoW method. This can give you a clear roadmap.

One of the most common mistakes I've seen when it comes to prioritization—both in startups and from PMs in established companies—is adding features based on assumptions rather than evidence. I made this mistake myself when I was a founder, thinking I knew best. It's easy to fall into the trap of believing a feature will add value simply because it sounds good in theory but without data and insights, whether qualitative or quantitative depending on your company's stage, you risk filling your roadmap with ideas that don't actually help your customers or drive meaningful results. Instead, these features can end up wasting your team's time and resources.

Feature prioritization matrix (Figure 2-4)

Imagine a four-quadrant graph. The X-axis (horizontal) represents "Effort" while the Y-axis (vertical) represents "Impact."

1. Quadrant I (top left): High Impact, Low Effort

2. Quadrant II (top right): High Impact, High Effort

3. Quadrant III (bottom left): Low Impact, Low Effort

4. Quadrant IV (bottom right): Low Impact, High Effort

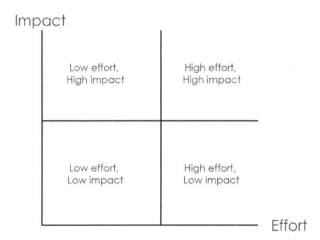

Figure 2-4. *Feature prioritization matrix*

Now, let's populate it with some hypothetical product features.

Sample features:

- User profile customization: Allow users to customize their profiles with themes.

- Instant chat: A live chat feature for customer support.

- Recommendation engine: Suggest products based on user browsing history.

- Multilanguage support: Introducing additional language options.

- Dark mode: A night theme for the app.

Placing the features on the matrix (Figure 2-5):

User profile customization:

- Effort: Medium (Some new graphics, minor backend changes)

- Impact: Low (Nice to have, but not necessarily impactful for the core experience)

Instant chat:

- Effort: Low (Third-party integrations available)

- Impact: High (Immediate help boosts user satisfaction)

Recommendation engine:

- Effort: High (Requires significant backend development and data analysis)

- Impact: High (Directly can lead to increased sales)

Multilanguage support:

- Effort: High (Translation, potential UI changes)
- Impact: Medium (Opens up to new markets but requires maintenance)

Dark mode:

- Effort: Low (Mainly UI changes)
- Impact: Medium (Improved user experience, especially for night users)

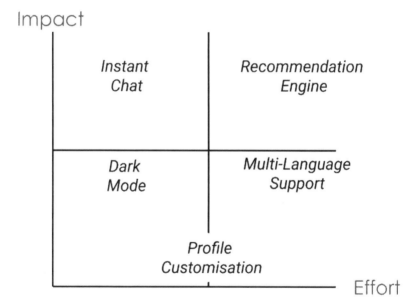

Figure 2-5. *Feature prioritization matrix example*

Analysis and decision:

Features in Quadrant I (High Impact, Low Effort) are your low-hanging fruits. You'd want to implement these first as they provide immediate value for relatively little work.

Quadrant II (High Impact, High Effort) features are long-term investments. They might be important, but you'll need to plan them carefully and make sure you have the resources.

Quadrant III (Low Impact, Low Effort) features can be implemented if you have spare resources, but they shouldn't be a priority.

Quadrant IV (Low Impact, High Effort) is tricky. These features might not offer much value for the effort they require. Evaluate if they align with your long-term strategy.

So, for our example, you might start with implementing the instant chat and the dark mode, then plan out the recommendation engine, and consider the user profile customization and multilanguage support based on resource availability.

Setting Timelines

When setting the timelines, it is important to account for everyone's availability, and make sure that no stage of the journey stops due to a person's absence. Break tasks down and allocate resources to allow an even distribution of the workload and maintain achievable deadlines.

A good way to break down engineering tasks to get to more reliable estimates (and deadlines) is to break them down until they can get done within one or a few days of development. This is because challenges could always arise and bigger estimates are never accurate.

Share the Roadmap with Stakeholders

Building a product is a collaborative task and much like in any team project, every stakeholder—from designers, analysts, and developers to marketers—has a key role to play. Make sure you talk about your roadmap, and keep everyone aligned so that you can understand the perspectives and concerns each party has. When you discuss with different people, you realize that each department, be it marketing, sales, or engineering, has its unique motivations. Some might be driven by revenue metrics, others by tech, and yet others by overall user experience.

When you actively involve stakeholders, you improve the alignment with them. Transparent roadmaps that detail current statuses and upcoming milestones can also alleviate their concerns. Use these as opportunities to educate stakeholders about specific product decisions, their reasoning, and outcomes.

If there's a change in direction or a reprioritization, it will be easy to communicate them, as surprises, especially in product, can lead to unnecessary friction.

CHAPTER 3

Stakeholder Management

Product management is a journey not to be taken alone. When stakeholders are aligned, they can significantly accelerate your product's success; however, if stakeholders aren't properly guided, they can divert your product off course and block its progress.

Stakeholder management involves the identification, analysis, and prioritization of those entities and people that significantly impact your mission's outcome.

They offer resources, important feedback, and, depending on your company, the green signal to progress. Whether internal, like your team and leadership, or external, like customers and investors, their actions can either create barriers or, if used correctly, open up new roads.

As we explore this chapter of our journey, we'll talk about the details of stakeholder management, sharing tools and tactics to help you manage through this aspect of the PM role:

1. **Understanding and Identifying Key Stakeholders:** Identify the key individuals who influence your product's success and learn how to engage them effectively.

2. **Dealing with Difficult Stakeholders:** Learn how to overcome challenges with difficult stakeholders to keep your product on track and maintain momentum.

© Michele Galli 2025
M. Galli, *Navigating the Product Galaxy*, https://doi.org/10.1007/979-8-8688-1148-7_3

3. **The RACI Model:** Clarify roles and responsibilities to improve team efficiency and create better collaboration.

Understanding and Identifying Key Stakeholders

Stakeholder management is a pillar of product management and it is about building trust with your stakeholders by making them well-informed about the product's direction, progress, challenges, and the rationale behind specific decisions.

Stakeholders can be internal teams, upper management, investors, or even key customers and play an important role in your product's success. Mismanaging stakeholders, I learned during the years, can quickly lead to a loss of trust and cause significant disruptions. Among them, the CEO is the most critical stakeholder of all for any PM. You should make sure that the product aligns with the CEO's vision and priorities.

How to Manage Stakeholder Expectations Effectively

In my experience, keeping stakeholders in the loop is much like maintaining strong relationships with friends or family. You don't tell everyone everything, but you make sure they know what they need to know, and you definitely keep them updated about big news.

So, first things first: keep things regular. Whether that's sending out an update every week, once a month, or even every quarter, sticking to a rhythm helps everyone know when to expect news. It's like how you might call your family on Sundays or catch up with a friend every couple of weeks.

Next, think about who you're talking to; just like you wouldn't go into work details with a friend who's not in your field, not every stakeholder needs every bit of information. For some, an overview is enough, while others might want to go into the specifics. I've learned that customizing messages to fit your audience keeps stakeholders engaged and also builds trust over time.

It's also important to create a forum for stakeholders to provide feedback. If you don't do this proactively, feedback will still come—but it might be in a more disruptive way. Creating regular touchpoints for feedback helps you stay ahead of potential issues and creates a more collaborative environment.

If there's a change in your project or a delay, it's good to give a heads up. Make sure to explain why it happened and, if possible, lay out the next steps or new plans. I've made the mistake of under-communicating changes before, and it's a lesson I wouldn't recommend learning the hard way. Clear updates can save you a lot of trouble.

Lastly, don't be afraid to say "I don't know, but I'll figure it out." Senior stakeholders can easily spot insincerity, and it's better to show honesty and a commitment to finding the answers than to risk losing credibility by pretending to know everything.

Identifying the Stakeholders

Every product's development is influenced by multiple voices but some are louder and hold more power over significant decisions. Identifying and understanding these stakeholders early on can make all the difference in how your product evolves.

One way to do it is to catalog all potential stakeholders and understand the influence and interest of each of them. High-influence individuals or groups can significantly change your product's direction as their buy-in is often needed for key decisions and can also be helpful in getting others on board.

At the same time, those with high interest, even if they don't have significant power, are your product's advocates. Their passion can provide a morale boost and sometimes, they can be the ones to spot potential opportunities that others might overlook.

Use a Power-Interest Matrix

This is a tool to map out your stakeholders based on their interest in your product and their influence in the organization and will help you tailor your communication.

How to create a power-interest grid (Table 3-1):

1. Add all stakeholders involved or affected by your project.

2. Rate their power on a scale of 1 to 10 (10 being most influential). Consider their role, control over resources, or ability to influence opinions.

3. Rate their interest on a scale of 1 to 10 (10 being most interested). Interest doesn't always equate to power.

4. Place each stakeholder on the grid based on their ratings.

Table 3-1. *Power-interest matrix*

Category	Actions
High Influence, High Interest	Regular detailed updates (possibly weekly). These are key decision-makers who are deeply involved.
High Influence, Low Interest	Less frequent, high-level updates (perhaps monthly) about major milestones or changes.
Low Influence, High Interest	Detailed updates but perhaps less frequently, maybe bi-weekly.
Low Influence, Low Interest	Occasional broad updates.

Engaging Your Stakeholders

When done effectively, product updates can turn passive observers into active contributors.

Three tips for great stakeholders' presentations:

- Golden circle: Use the "golden circle" principle, famously introduced by Simon Sinek, and consistently loop back to the "why" of your product as the core purpose often resonates most with stakeholders, reminding them of the larger mission.

- The 10-20-30 rule: One hack for a good engagement for your presentation is the "10-20-30 Rule" by Guy Kawasaki: A presentation should have no more than 10 slides, last no longer than 20 minutes, and use a font size of no less than 30 points.

- The 5/15 rule: Provide a synopsis of your story in 5 minutes, intriguing enough to draw people into a deeper 15-minute exploration.

CASE STUDY: FINTECH INNOVATIONS INC.

FinTech Innovations Inc., a fintech startup, was preparing for the launch of their payment gateway, to simplify cross-border transactions. The product manager Carla was responsible for the task of ensuring that all stakeholders, both internal and external, were aligned with the product's vision, features, and launch strategy.

She had a big spectrum of stakeholders, the tech team wanted technical details and frequent updates; investors wanted assurances of progress and returns; the marketing team needed to be in the know to strategize the market launch; and the sales team was keen on product knowledge to pitch to potential clients. Carla understood a one-size-fits-all communication approach would be ineffective.

To tackle this challenge, she decided to use the high-interest matrix and conducted one-on-one interviews with representatives from each stakeholder group to understand their interest levels and the type of information they required.

Tech team and investors (High Influence, High Interest): Carla scheduled weekly sync-up meetings. For the tech team, she went deep into the product's technical features, bug reports, and addressed any development bottlenecks. For the investors, she prepared a weekly dashboard showing progress against the milestones, potential risks, and mitigation plans.

Marketing team (High Influence, Low Interest): Carla organized bi-weekly sessions and provided them with high-level overviews, focusing on product USPs, target audience demographics, and expected market penetration. She also collaborated with them on planning the launch event.

Sales team (Low Influence, High Interest): They were given a monthly product training session, including hands-on product demos and selling point workshops. Additionally, Carla shared success stories from beta testers, which the sales team could use as testimonials.

THE GOLDEN CIRCLE: START WITH WHY

The golden circle (Figure 3-1) is a concept introduced by Simon Sinek, a leadership expert and author, and it's a principle that explains why some organizations and individuals are more innovative, influential, and profitable than others. This concept helped me greatly from early in my career, and I consider it one of the most important concepts in product management. Understanding and applying the golden circle can significantly improve your approach to product management, and help you create products that truly resonate with your customers.

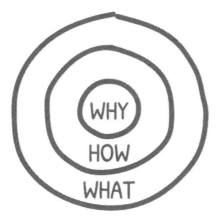

Figure 3-1. *Golden circle*

1. Why

   At the core of the circle is the "Why" and represents the purpose, cause, or belief that drives every one of us. It's the reason an organization exists beyond just making money and it is the foundation of an organization's or individual's belief system. It's what inspires people to take action, be it buying a product or joining a movement. In Sinek's words, it's about "why you do what you do."

   For example, Apple's "Why" is often stated as their belief in challenging the status quo and thinking differently.

2. How

   The next layer out is the "How." This refers to the processes, values, or principles that guide how an organization realizes its "Why." It's about the unique value proposition, the differentiators that set you apart from competitors.

Using Apple again, their "How" can be thought of as their commitment to user-friendly design and innovative technology.

3. What

The outermost circle represents the "What." It's the tangible products, services, or results that an organization delivers. It's often the most visible aspect of an organization, but without the underlying "Why" and "How," it lacks depth and emotional connection.

In Apple's case, their "What" includes products like iPhones, MacBooks, and iPads.

Significance and application

Most organizations start with "What" and then move inward to "How" and, sometimes, even "Why." However, Sinek argues that the most influential and inspiring leaders and organizations think and act the opposite way: they start with "Why."

By starting with the "Why," organizations can tap into the emotional drivers behind consumer behavior. When consumers believe in an organization's "Why," they're not just buying a product; they're buying into a belief or a cause. This creates a deeper level of loyalty and can turn customers into brand advocates.

When using the golden circle in presentations and documentations, particularly for product managers, it can serve as a framework to

- State the core belief or purpose behind a product or feature, why does it exist, and why should anyone care.

- Next, show how this vision is realized, what strategies, technologies, or principles are being employed.

- Finally, present the tangible outcome. By the time the audience sees this, they already understand its significance and the values driving it.

Dealing with Difficult Stakeholders

Every product manager, be it a seasoned PM or a newbie, will have to deal with challenging stakeholders. These people may be resistant to change, overly critical, or have contrasting views on the product's direction and can disrupt the morale of a team, and no one wants a work environment filled with tension.

When working with them, pause, absorb, and actively listen to understand what's behind their words. Are they driven by past experiences? Do they have personal stakes that are yet to surface? One lesson I learned is that by taking the time to really understand the underlying motivations of a difficult stakeholder, it often reveals concerns that hadn't been openly communicated, which will enable you to effectively resolve them.

You should adjust your communication to each stakeholder as some individuals resonate with data-driven arguments, while others might be attracted by the vision of the future and changing our message based on these differences can bridge opposing views.

Criticism, while sometimes hard to swallow, especially when directed at a project we're passionate about, can be a good chance to grow and instead of adopting a defensive stance, you can use feedback to guide your efforts. A costly mistake I've seen teams make is to dismiss critical feedback too quickly. Embracing the feedback, on the other hand, has often led to significant improvements and by inviting stakeholders to propose solutions, you can change the narrative from problem-spotting to collaborative problem-solving, creating a united front focused on success.

The Reframing Technique

Often, conflicts come from differences in perspective rather than in objectives and the way someone perceives an issue can influence their response to it. When dealing with difficult stakeholders, "reframing" the problem can be a powerful tool.

Reframing is essentially the act of shifting the narrative or changing the lens through which a particular issue is viewed. It's presenting a situation in a new light, making it more palatable or highlighting different aspects that might resonate better with the stakeholder's concerns.

I've found that reframing a challenging conversation by aligning it with a stakeholder's primary concerns often diffuses tension and opens up more productive dialogue. For example, if a stakeholder is resistant to a new feature because they believe it will over-complicate the user interface, you might reframe the conversation by discussing how this feature aligns with user feedback, or how it offers a competitive edge in the market. Alternatively, you could highlight how, with adequate training and support, users can quickly benefit from the new feature.

Using this technique, you acknowledge the stakeholder's concerns while providing a different angle, allowing both of you to find common ground and work toward a solution. This approach has helped me transform many adversarial relationships into collaborative ones, focusing people on the shared goal of product success.

CASE STUDY: GREENSCAPE TECH

GreenScape Tech was a company working on sustainable innovation and their commitment to pushing the boundaries of eco-friendly technology was unmatched in the industry. Yet, within GreenScape's walls was Mr. Peters, a stakeholder with a reputation that preceded him. People often felt the weight of his skeptical opinions.

Sarah, the lead product manager at GreenScape, recognizing the obstacle, decided that understanding the man behind the skepticism was the first step. Sarah believed in the power of casual, open conversation—a contrast to the formal confines of a boardroom and over coffee, Sarah chatted with Mr. Peters in candid discussions.

It was during one of these conversations that Sarah discovered a defining moment in Mr. Peters' past where he had once championed an innovative project, which, due to complications, didn't see the light of day. This failure shook his confidence in innovation.

Sarah knew that to win Mr. Peters' trust, she needed to provide tangible evidence of progress. She used prototypes to allow Mr. Peters to see ideas in their initial stage, giving him a sense of assurance.

Sarah then started hosting bi-weekly sessions, where the team would show their small yet significant victories and celebrated each milestone showcasing the progress they were making. This kept Mr. Peters informed and made him feel involved, valued, and heard. With each prototype and milestone, Mr. Peters started showing optimism and went from highlighting risks to suggesting improvements.

The path of product management isn't always about the product itself; often, it's about the people who shape its destiny. Sarah's approach recognized the stakeholder's experiences shaping his perspective and aligning them with the company's vision. When we take the time to understand and listen, we create the way for success, collaboration, and innovation.

The RACI Model

You're leading a team that is eager and capable, but if each member isn't clear on their exact role, you might find yourself caught in confusion or worse—stuck in endless meetings! The RACI model clarifies who does what, so everyone isn't trying to steer the project at once.

Let's look at the breakdown:

- Responsible (R): The team members directly executing the tasks. They're on the frontline and get the work done.

- Accountable (A): The person ensuring everything is on track. They're answerable for the task's outcome. It's important to have one person in this role to avoid confusion.

- Consulted (C): The experts whose insights you seek before making important decisions. Their input guides the process, helping to avoid potential issues.

- Informed (I): Those who need updates on progress but aren't directly involved in the task execution. They stay informed to prepare for what comes next.

Imagine launching a new feature in your app. The developers (R) are coding it, the product manager (A) ensures it aligns with the vision, UX designers (C) give feedback on usability, and the marketing team (I) is kept in the loop for their campaign.

RACI template

Sketch a simple table (Table 3-2). Tasks or decisions down the side and stakeholders across the top. Assign each with an R, A, C, or I. Voila! You've got a clear responsibility map for your product.

Table 3-2. RACI

Tasks/Decisions	Product Manager	Developers	UX Designers	Sales Team
Finalizing feature requirements	A, R	C	C	I
Developing the actual feature	C	R	I	I
Testing feature functionality	C	R	C	I
Gathering user feedback	A	I	R	C
Sales pitch preparation based on the feature	C	I	C	R
Post-launch analysis and improvements	A, R	C	R	C

Key:

- R (Responsible)—Person(s) who execute the task.

- A (Accountable)—Person(s) responsible for the final outcome.

- C (Consulted)—Person(s) who provide valuable inputs.

- I (Informed)—Person(s) who need to be kept updated.

CHAPTER 4

User Research and Product Metrics

As product managers, aligning our vision with user needs is the most important thing we can do, and in this chapter, we'll look into the heart of understanding our users. We'll uncover techniques to connect with them, discover their needs, and create products that meet these needs.

Here's what we will cover in this chapter:

1. **User Interviews and Their Power:** Discover how talking to users can reveal insights that shape the future of your product based on real needs and feedback.

2. **Surveys and Questionnaires:** Master the art of designing effective surveys, collecting meaningful data, and analyzing feedback to extract actionable insights that drive product decisions.

3. **User Persona Creation:** Learn the process of building detailed user personas that serve as guides for making product decisions rooted in a deep understanding of your audience.

4. **User Story Mapping:** Visualize and map out the user journey to identify key touchpoints and improve the overall user experience.

© Michele Galli 2025
M. Galli, *Navigating the Product Galaxy*, https://doi.org/10.1007/979-8-8688-1148-7_4

5. **A/B Testing in Product:** Explore data-driven methods to improve your product, using A/B testing to compare variations, optimize design, and make informed decisions.

6. **How to Increase Conversion Rates:** Discover proven strategies to increase conversion rates across your product, and learn how to steer clear of common mistakes.

7. **Key Product Metrics:** Understand how to identify and track the most important metrics, leveraging data to refine your product strategy.

User Interviews and Their Power

User interviews, when done correctly, reveal great insights into the user's problems, offering a clearer understanding of their world. Some of the most unexpected insights often come from these conversations, where users reveal challenges that hadn't been anticipated.

Setting the Scene

Think of setting the scene for a user interview like laying the foundation for a building, the stability and success of everything that comes after depends on this initial step.

Select the right environment as it sets the tone and, whether you're in a physical space or a digital one, it should be welcoming. A well-lit room can make the user feel relaxed. If you're meeting virtually, consider using a virtual background that isn't distracting.

Before going into the core questions, have a little casual small talk to break the ice, ask them how their day is going, or share a light observation from yours. This approach has often led me to more open and honest conversations, making users feel more comfortable and willing to share their true thoughts.

Always be prepared. If you're on a video call, make sure there is a good connection for both of you and share any links or documents they might need in advance as technical issues can sometimes disrupt the flow. It's always a good idea to do a quick audio and video check before you get into the interview.

Remember to respect your interviewee's time and stick to the duration you've informed them about. No one likes sessions that drag on, so be conscious of the clock and yet, while you're mindful of time, also reassure them that there's no rush—you genuinely want to hear what they have to say.

Never forget to reiterate why you're both here and give them a brief reminder about the purpose of the conversation to make them feel their feedback is valued.

Asking the Right Questions

Kick things off with a broad scope to allow users to comfortably get into the discussion before you get into the details. For example, questions like "tell me about your overall experience with our app" or "how does our product fit into your daily activities" set a friendly tone and can naturally lead into more areas of discussion.

One of the essential techniques is to frame questions that open doors to expansive answers, rather than those that end with a simple yes or no.

Think of it this way, rather than asking if they liked a movie, ask what parts of the movie resonated with them the most. Instead of wondering if they found your checkout process simple, look into their experience during the checkout.

But don't stop at just getting answers; ask users to tell you about their experiences and prompt them with questions like, "can you remember a particular moment with our platform that stands out?" or "describe an example where something didn't feel right."

Another way to do it is to ask them to walk you through their steps when they try to complete a task. For example, "imagine it's the end of the month, and you need to send money to your parents living in your home country. Can you please walk me through the process?"

However, always remain an unbiased interviewer as it's easy to ask leading questions, especially when you're eager for positive feedback. It might be tempting to ask, "you enjoyed the new update, right?" but it's way better to keep it neutral with, "How did you perceive the recent update?"

There was a time when I was conducting user interviews for a new feature we had just rolled out and I was eager to hear positive feedback, so I asked, "you found the new dashboard better than it was a while ago, right?" The interviewee nodded and agreed, but I later realized that by phrasing the question this way, I had led them to a positive response. When I reviewed the session afterward, I noticed that I had missed the opportunity to hear their unfiltered thoughts. It turned out that the user actually had some confusion with the new layout, which only came to light when I dug deeper in later interviews with more neutral questions.

If a user mentions a specific feature or problem, don't be afraid to ask further. "You mentioned the search function; can you elaborate on that?" It's here that you often find the most valuable insights.

Another effective technique is to review user data to verify their reported actions. If you find discrepancies between what users say and what they do, it might indicate a potential issue with comprehension. I remember a situation where users reported loving a feature, but the data showed it was almost never used. That discrepancy led us to go deeper into why the customers told us otherwise and discovered they thought we were talking about a different feature.

The Power of Silence

In our daily life, we often underestimate the power of silence; however, when it comes to user interviews, silence becomes one of the most useful tools in your arsenal.

In interviews, the silent gaps emphasize the words that come after, so when a user has just shared a piece of feedback or talked about an experience, avoid jumping in immediately, either with a response or another question.

Instead, give it a breath and allow a few seconds of quiet to permeate the conversation. This does a couple of things.

Firstly, it gives your interviewee a chance to reflect on what they've just said and often in these moments, they go deeper, adding layers to their initial thoughts, or even bringing up something entirely new that they hadn't considered in their initial response.

Secondly, it tells your user that you're genuinely listening, that you're giving weight to their words and processing them. It makes them feel valued, they recognize they have the floor, and what they say next might be even more insightful.

However, using silence as a tool requires practice. Too little, and you might cut off potential insights, too much and it can become awkward, making the user question whether they've said something weird.

You should also understand the user's comfort level. If they seem to be struggling or growing increasingly uncomfortable with the silence, it's your cue to move forward.

Be Curious, Not Leading

When interviewing, you should approach the conversation with a genuine desire to learn, and while it's important to be curious, it's equally important not to let your biases guide the conversation.

During user interviews, leading questions can steer the user's responses in a direction that matches your assumptions and instead of getting unbiased insights, you might end up with feedback that's been influenced by your line of questioning.

Ensuring you're not leading the conversation does require a degree of self-awareness and as product managers it's natural to have some level of attachment or bias toward our creations. But it's this very attachment that we need to be careful of during interviews.

To avoid leading questions:

1. Before the interview, review your questions to leave out anything that might be leading. It's a simple step, but it can make a world of difference. Use pilot interviews and initial feedback to refine your questions.

2. Instead of thinking about your next question, truly listen to the user. Their feedback can guide the conversation organically.

3. Even if you think you know where the user is headed with their response, give them the space to finish as you might be surprised by the turns their narrative takes.

4. Stay aware of non-verbal cues as they can provide insights into the user's comfort level and whether they feel they're being led or genuinely listened to.

Surveys and Questionnaires

Discovery doesn't end with user interviews, surveys and questionnaires can open up to a lot of insights. In fact, PMs and researchers often conduct user interviews first to collect insights and identify patterns that help in drawing up the survey questions and answers. In this way you make sure the survey is grounded in real user experiences and targets the right areas for exploration.

Starting Broad, Then Narrowing Down

Imagine the initial stages of your survey as a gentle handhold, guiding your respondents. Kick off with warm-up questions to ease them into the topic.

For example, if you're exploring feedback on a fitness app, a question like "how often do you exercise in a week?" works wonders as it's a soft intro, setting the tone for deeper conversations later on. These questions can also provide an early segmentation of your respondents as someone who exercises daily might have a different perspective than an occasional gym-goer.

As you go into it further, transition into the heart of what you want to know. Questions like "what features do you frequently use in our fitness app?" or "is there a specific workout regime you wish were available?" will now feel natural to the respondent as they've already shared their broader habits.

Toward the end, when the respondent is engaged, ask the more challenging or open-ended questions. For example, you can ask questions like "what improvements would you suggest for our app?" or "describe a time where our app played an important role in your fitness journey." I remember a survey where I front-loaded too many complex questions, and the response rate dropped significantly very quickly. Learning from that, I started designing surveys that always gradually build in complexity.

Sequencing here is the key as the flow of questions should feel logical, almost like a conversation gradually evolving. If it's a lengthy survey, you could show a progress indicator to give respondents a sense of how much longer they'll be engaged. Also, while open-ended questions yield rich data, distribute them wisely. Too many, and you risk overwhelming the respondent.

Clarity Above All

Confusing questions lead to confused answers, so you should be as clear and concise as possible. A clear survey respects your respondent's time and provides accurate answers.

Avoid industry-specific terms as, while you might be comfortable throwing around phrases like "UX improvements," a good portion of the general public might be left scratching their heads; instead, opt for more universally understood wording, like "improvements to how you use our app or website."

Vague questions can often lead respondents down unclear paths, resulting in skewed results. Once, while conducting a survey for a newly launched feature in our app, I included a question asking users about their "overall satisfaction" with the feature. The question was too broad—some users responded with feedback about the feature's interface, others about its performance, and a few even mentioned unrelated aspects like customer support. Because the question wasn't specific enough, the responses were all over the place, making it terribly hard to draw actionable insights. I learned from this that it's important to break down satisfaction into specific areas, like "ease of use" or "performance speed," to get more focused and useful feedback.

Another thing to avoid is the double-barreled question—questions that touch upon multiple issues but allow for just one answer. Imagine asking, "how satisfied are you with our product's price and quality?" It's problematic as someone might like the price but feel indifferent about the quality. How should they respond?

The format of your responses matters too. For example, if you're providing multiple-choice options, make sure each choice is distinct and self-explanatory and someone responding to a satisfaction scale from 1–5 should instantly understand what each number means.

Mixing It Up

While closed-ended questions (like multiple-choice or yes/no questions) are more straightforward to analyze, open-ended questions can provide better insights.

Think about the narrative you're presenting to your participants and begin with simpler questions—like multiple choice or rating scales—to warm them up. These types of questions are user-friendly, don't require much time, and give participants a sense of accomplishment right from the get-go. Once you've built some trust, add more open-ended questions. These questions allow for more depth and they offer participants the freedom to express themselves, and while they might take a little longer to analyze, they often provide rich insights that can be missed by fixed-response questions. After the open-ended questions, return to some of the quicker formats.

In one project, I noticed that open-ended questions toward the end of the survey yielded better insights compared to those placed in the middle. Respondents, even though they were fewer, were more invested by that point, leading to more detailed responses.

Be also mindful of sorting questions so that the more important ones are at the front of the survey. This way, even if users drop off midway, you still obtain valuable responses.

Avoiding Bias and Assumptions

As with interviews, your questions shouldn't lead respondents to a particular answer. It's tempting to frame questions positively about your product, but this can skew results.

Even the choices you offer as responses can be tricky ground. Let's say you're seeking opinions on a product's features; if you only list a handful of them, you're indirectly telling your users that these are the only ones that matter, potentially missing out on insights on features you didn't list. Good options, complemented by an "other" category where they can specify, can solve this issue.

Iterate, Iterate, Iterate

The first draft of your survey won't be perfect, and that's okay, start with a clear purpose in mind and define what you want to achieve from the survey before drafting your questions. To maintain focus, always ask, "what would I do with this insight, in the short or medium-term?" as this question helps make each survey question actionable.

Consider the first time you roll out a survey, the response rate might be low, or the feedback could be less insightful than anticipated. Discouraging? Perhaps. But in these moments, each block is an opportunity in disguise.

For example, in one survey I conducted, the response rate was much lower than expected. We realized the survey was too long and had been sent out during a busy period for our target demographic. After shortening the survey and rescheduling its release, the response rate improved significantly.

Don't overlook the feedback itself. I remember another time when we weren't getting the depth of insight we needed. We were asking questions like, "How do you feel about the navigation experience?" which led to vague responses like "It's okay" or "Could be better." After reviewing, we realized these questions were too open-ended and complex for what we wanted to learn. We simplified the question to something more specific, like "How easy is it to find the 'Contact Us' section?" with a 1–5 scale for responses. This led to much more valuable responses, such as "It took me a while to find it because it's buried in a submenu," which directly helped us identify the pain point and make improvements in the next iteration.

Closing the Loop

End your survey with an open invitation for any additional feedback, as sometimes this space can yield some of the most valuable insights and it's unrestricted by specific questions. But sending out your survey doesn't quite complete the circle. Instead, receiving, interpreting, and acting upon the feedback is where the magic really happens, so make sure participants don't feel their voice remains unheard.

From Data to Insights

To trust the quantitative side of the survey, you need a minimum number of responses. For example, for a population of 10,000, you would need a minimum of 370 responses to be 95% confident that the metric you want to measure has only a 5% margin of error (you can check the calculation through any sample size calculator on the Internet). By collecting an adequate number of responses, you can ensure the reliability and validity of your survey findings.

Once you've collected your responses, the real work begins. Look for patterns, contradictions, and surprises and transform raw data into actionable insights.

Collecting a large volume of data is one thing, but going through that to find insights is another. To start, familiarize yourself with the responses and spend time reading through the data. Once you have done that, segment your data and group similar responses together. Whether they're concerns about a specific feature, praises about the user experience, or suggestions, these categories help in spotting patterns.

When you find outliers or unique pieces of feedback that don't seem to fit anywhere, don't disregard them. While it's easy to focus on dominant trends, sometimes, these outliers can help identify issues or new ideas that aren't on the mainstream radar yet.

As insights begin to form, prioritize them, which issues are most pressing and which suggestions align with your brand's vision? Establishing a hierarchy helps in determining action steps versus long-term considerations.

To improve the accuracy of your insights, you should cross-check survey responses with existing data. Comparing survey results with behavioral data helps validate your insights and uncover hidden trends, leading to more informed decisions.

CASE STUDY: STREAMFLOW

StreamFlow, a music streaming service, started to notice a slight but consistent drop in their active users. Eager to understand the reasons behind this drop and find a solution, they segmented their users into three distinct categories: regular active users, users whose activity was declining, and users who had become inactive.

StreamFlow sent out brief, personalized surveys to their active user base with questions to understand satisfaction levels and any potential improvements, even amongst happy users. For example, "are there any features you wish StreamFlow had?" or "how would you describe our platform to a friend?"

Declining activity users received surveys designed to understand the friction points. The questions went into the reasons for their decreased usage, such as "what features of other platforms appeal to you?" or "have you experienced any challenges with StreamFlow recently?"

Inactive users were reached out with a mix of open-ended questions and multiple-choice formats to minimize the survey fatigue. They wanted to uncover the primary reasons behind users abandoning the platform. They included options like "found a better alternative," "faced technical issues," or "preferred music genres not available."

From the responses, StreamFlow found several key insights. Many users felt that while the platform lacked genres like classical, jazz, and world music, some pointed out the user interface was less intuitive than that of competitors, while others liked unique features, like lyrics popping up as songs played but found them tricky to navigate.

Reacting to the insights, StreamFlow expanded its musical offerings, forming partnerships with labels that specialized in underrepresented genres, redesigned the UI and reworked features like the lyrics display.

The fruits of their labor weren't far off as in the months after, StreamFlow reversed the decline of its active users and registered a 15% increase in new subscriptions.

SURVEY TIPS AND TECHNIQUES

Question types

- Likert scale: This is a common way to understand sentiments. Questions like "On a scale from 1 to 5, how satisfied are you with our mobile app?" can provide quantifiable data on user feelings.

- Ranking questions: When wanting to prioritize features or options, use ranking. "Rank the following features from 1 to 5 based on importance to you: A, B, C, D, E."

- Semantic differential: Instead of agreeing or disagreeing, users choose between two opposite adjectives, like "Is the user interface intuitive or confusing?"

The power of piping

Modern survey tools allow you to use respondents' previous answers to change subsequent questions. If a respondent mentions they use an iPhone, the next questions can go deeper into their iOS experience.

Time and duration

Always be mindful of the respondent's time and a quick note at the beginning, such as "This survey will take approximately 10 minutes of your time," sets expectations.

A personal touch

Even in a digital survey, a touch of personalization can increase completion rates. Address the respondent by name, if possible, or tailor questions based on user demographics to make the survey feel less generic.

Incentivizing responses

Sometimes, a little incentive can boost participation, whether it's a discount, entry into a giveaway, or just a thank-you note.

The rule of one

Similar to user interviews, each question should aim to extract one piece of information. Avoid double-barreled questions and break them down into separate questions.

Respect privacy

If you're collecting personal data, make sure respondents know why you're collecting it, how it will be used, and that their data is safe.

User Persona Creation

User personas are composite representations made up of common behaviors, goals, and pain points of various users.

Personas provide teams with a clear understanding of whom they're designing for and by creating these user profiles, product designers, analysts, and developers make sure their decisions serve the users' genuine needs.

Identifying the Need for Personas

While the concept of user personas is not new in the world of product management, their implementation isn't universal. Not every project or product will get the same benefits from user personas, and sometimes, their creation might even be superfluous. So, how do you know if you need personas?

To start, consider the scope and complexity of the project. If you're designing a landing page or a simple website with limited interactivity, spending time on personas might not give you a proportionate return on investment. However, the scales tip in favor of personas when you're dealing with multiple platforms or applications, especially those targeting a wide range of needs.

Secondly, think about the user's journey. Is the journey linear, with few touchpoints? Or is it complex, demanding user choices and interactions at multiple stages? For the latter, personas can be useful in optimizing each touchpoint with the users' needs.

Another consideration is the diversity of the audience. If your audience is homogeneous, with consistent behavior and needs, personas may be redundant, but if you serve multiple groups with distinct expectations, personas become a good tool to keep the design and product decisions aligned with individual user segments.

Project resources and time frame also play a role, and while it's rarely advisable to skip user research (unless you already have a good understanding of the user), there are projects with tight deadlines or limited resources where other user-centered research methods might take precedence. Here, you could use quick-and-dirty proto-personas, based on assumptions and/or existing understandings of the users rather than detailed research.

Collecting the Data

Begin with user interviews to understand your target audience as interviews let you understand the customers' daily lives, routines, and the context in which they'd use what you offer. Their stories, hopes, and pain points will serve as the foundation of your personas.

Surveys are the next logical step and through them, you can capture demographics, habits, preferences, and more. If your product is already out there, look into its analytics as the paths users take, the features they love, the points where they drop off paint a picture of user intent and areas of friction.

You should also look at platforms like X (formerly Twitter) and Reddit and go through support tickets. Within your organization, stakeholders and especially those in client-facing roles can provide stories and experiences that can add another layer of depth to your personas.

Creating the Persona

Start with a narrative. For example, "Emma, a busy single mother of two, seeks hassle-free online shopping experiences due to her hectic schedule." This story provides a more vivid picture than just demographics. Attach also a symbolic photo or illustration, while the image is representative, it makes the persona come alive, encouraging empathy within the team.

No persona is complete without demographic data like age, gender, profession, location, and education of the persona as it helps the team visualize where this persona fits within the larger user ecosystem. It's also important to identify the persona's daily routines, preferences, and motivations. Is Emma tech-savvy? Does she prioritize convenience or affordability?

Every user interacts with a product with specific goals in mind. Emma might approach an online store to find products, obtain information, or find special deals. These goals, along with the challenges or obstacles she faces, can give areas of opportunity.

To further humanize the persona, add some personal details—maybe Emma loves weekend hikes or hates pop-up ads. While not directly impacting product design, these bits add depth. You can also add real user quotes into the persona narrative, to give it a voice.

Don't forget to touch upon the user's journey with your product, whether Emma is a regular shopper, an occasional visitor, or a newbie, her interaction pattern provides good cues.

Multiple Personas for Multiple Users

Every product or service, regardless of its nature, serves a diverse user base with different needs, preferences, and behaviors and a single persona cannot contain this entire spectrum.

Consider a product like a digital news app. There's Mark, the morning commuter, going through headlines during his subway ride, then there's Sophia, a college student, who goes deep into opinion pieces late at night. Each has unique behaviors, motivations, and interaction patterns with the app.

While your product might have thousands of users, they can often be segmented into distinct groups based on commonalities. For example, frequency of use, specific features they gravitate toward, or the challenges they face can be starting points to segment them.

Personas can highlight potential areas of improvements or even entirely new features. For example, if you recognize Mark's need to consume news quickly, it might lead you to work on a feature that curates top headlines; on the other hand, acknowledging Sophia's reading habits might result in a "save for later" feature.

Creating personas, however, shouldn't complicate your product and you shouldn't try to cover for every possible need. I learned this the hard way. In a previous project, we ended up creating a dozen personas, thinking we were covering all possible user types. This diluted our focus, and we found ourselves trying to please every persona, which resulted in a product that didn't fully satisfy any of them. Now, I focus on prioritizing the most critical user groups or those whose needs are underserved, which helps maintain a clear direction with the team and ultimately leads to a better product.

CASE STUDY: FITLIFE

FitLife, an app designed to provide workout routines and nutrition plans, had initial success due to its database of exercises; however, over time, user engagement started to decrease. Sales and support feedback suggested users loved the content, but something was off and the FitLife team believed it was time for a revamp, with user personas at the center of this transformation.

FitLife's initial success had brought in a diverse user base, from fitness enthusiasts to beginners trying to adopt a healthier lifestyle. But while this diversity was a strength, it also became a challenge as the one-size-fits-all approach that had been so effective initially was no longer useful.

To understand the needs of their users, FitLife conducted a series of interviews with current users, past users, and potential users. At the same time, they also analyzed the user interactions, including session durations, frequently visited sections, features used, and more.

The team identified four primary user groups:

- "Fitness fanatics": Experienced gym-goers looking for advanced routines.

- "The transformers": Individuals on a weight loss or muscle gain program.

- "Wellness warriors": Those focused on holistic wellness, including both exercise and mindful practices.

- "Beginners": Newbies looking for guided plans and motivation.

Using these personas, FitLife began redesigning its app interface and content and introduced tiered workout plans serving each persona. For the wellness warriors, they introduced a meditation section, while the beginners received a gamified motivation system to keep them engaged.

Post revamp, FitLife saw a 30% increase in user engagement within three months. Their retention rates improved, and the user reviews showed the personal touch they felt with the app.

User Story Mapping

User Story Mapping (USM) is a visual exercise that improves your team's understanding of the user journey, ensuring everyone is aligned. USM breaks down the big picture (your product vision) into manageable chunks (user stories), creating a cohesive narrative of how users interact with your product.

Visualizing the Journey As a Narrative Arc

Imagine creating a storyboard for a film where each frame represents a moment in your user's interaction with your product. User story mapping does the same for your product development process by laying out the entire user experience on a canvas, where every action, every click, and every decision your user makes is a scene in this narrative. This visualization helps in identifying what your users are doing, why they're doing it, what motivates them, and what frustrates them.

The beauty of user story mapping lies in its user-centric approach as it explores the users' mindset, their needs and pain points. By mapping out their journey, you're tracking a series of interactions with a digital interface while you're putting together a story of their experiences, expectations, and emotions. It's a process that requires empathy and insight, as you're essentially writing the story of your user's day-to-day interactions with your product.

Creating Your Map

When creating your map, define the ultimate goal of your user's interaction with the product as this goal guides every other element.

Once the goal is set, identify the major activities or broad steps the user takes to achieve this goal. These activities are like milestones in the user's journey with your product. For example, in an e-commerce app, these might be browsing products, adding items to a cart, and completing a purchase.

The next layer of detail involves breaking down these activities into smaller, more specific tasks. Each task represents an action users take within each activity. In the e-commerce example, tasks under browsing products might be selecting product categories, applying filters, or viewing product details.

These tasks should be arranged in a logical order that reflects the natural progression of the user's journey so that the user's path through your product is intuitive.

It's also important to ground your map in real user data to make sure the map accurately represents how users actually interact with your product, rather than how you think they should. It happened to me a few times, where we mapped out what we thought was the perfect user journey, only to discover through analytics that users were consistently dropping off at a point we hadn't anticipated. It's always a humbling reminder that data often tells a different story than assumptions do and incorporating conversion and drop-off data can provide better insights into which parts of the journey are more challenging than others. The combination of qualitative mapping with quantitative data helps to identify specific points where users may find issues highlighting user challenges, quantifying them and helping your team to prioritize improvements more effectively.

Overall, the map you create highlights the key activities and tasks users do and presents them in an ordered, logical sequence and it serves as a guiding framework for your team, helping everyone understand the user experience and how each part of the product contributes to achieving the overall goal. The user story mapping pushes you to step into the shoes of your users and to see your product as a part of someone's daily routine, understanding their challenges, needs, and motivations.

Aligning with Business Goals

User story mapping offers a high-level view of a project and helps teams see how each feature fits into the bigger picture. This perspective is important for decision-makers and stakeholders, as it links user needs directly to business outcomes and helps identify which features are essential for delivering value to the user while also driving key business metrics, such as user engagement, customer retention, or revenue growth.

If you want to know more about user story mapping, there is a great book about it: *User Story Mapping* by Jeff Patton. You can also check a USM template in Table 4-1 and a practical example in Table 4-2.

USER STORY MAPPING TEMPLATE

Table 4-1. *User story mapping template*

Stage	Activity 1	Activity 2	Activity 3
User Goals	Goal A	Goal B	Goal C
User Tasks	Task A1	Task B1	Task C1
	Task A2	Task B2	Task C2
User Actions	Action A1	Action B1	Action C1
	Action A2	Action B2	Action C2
Pain Points	Pain Point A	Pain Point B	Pain Point C
Opportunities	Opportunity A	Opportunity B	Opportunity C

Explanation of the table:

- Stage: This column categorizes the information into different stages of the user journey, like User Goals, User Tasks, User Actions, Pain Points, and Opportunities.

- Activity 1, 2, 3: These columns represent different user activities or steps in the user journey. Each activity is broken down into tasks and actions.

- User Goals: These are the high-level objectives that the user wants to achieve with each activity.

- User Tasks: These are smaller tasks that make up each activity. They are the specific things users need to do to accomplish their goals.

- User Actions: These are the actions users take while performing each task.

- Pain Points: This section identifies challenges or problems users face at each stage of the activity.

- Opportunities: This section suggests potential improvements or solutions to improve the user experience.

A Practical Example

Table 4-2. *User story mapping example*

Stage	Activity 1: Browsing products	Activity 2: Adding to cart	Activity 3: Checkout
User Goals	Find desired products	Select items for purchase	Complete purchase easily
User Tasks	Navigate to product category	Review product details	Enter shipping information
	Filter and sort products	Add items to cart	Choose payment method
User Actions	Click on category	Read product descriptions	Fill in address details
	Apply filters and sort options	Click "Add to Cart" button	Select payment option
Pain Points	Difficulty finding categories	Unclear product information	Complicated payment process
	Overwhelming number of options	No quick add-to-cart feature	Too many form fields
Opportunities	Improve category navigation	Improve product descriptions	Simplify payment process
	Implement better filtering	Add a quick add-to-cart button	Reduce number of form fields

Activity 1: Browsing products

- Goal: Users want to find products they are interested in.

- Tasks and actions: They navigate to different categories and use filters to narrow down choices.

- Pain points: Users find it hard to locate specific categories and feel overwhelmed by choices.

- Opportunities: Improving category navigation and filtering options.

Activity 2: Adding to cart

- Goal: Users want to select items for purchase.

- Tasks and actions: They review product details and add items to their cart.

- Pain points: Product information is sometimes unclear, and there's no quick way to add items to the cart.

- Opportunities: Improving product descriptions and adding a quick add-to-cart feature.

Activity 3: Checkout

- Goal: Users want to complete their purchase easily and quickly.

- Tasks and actions: They enter shipping details and choose a payment method.

- Pain points: The payment process is complicated with too many form fields.

- Opportunities: Simplifying the payment process and reducing the number of form fields.

A/B Testing in Product

A/B testing involves presenting two variants (A and B) of a particular element of your product to your user base to test a specific hypothesis and analyze which one performs better. The goal is to make data-driven decisions that improve the user experience, engagement, and conversion rates.

When to Use A/B Testing

A/B testing is a great tool when you want to minimize the risk associated with changes to your product. It helps in understanding the impact of a change before rolling it out to your entire user base, avoiding potential negative effects on user experience or business metrics.

This method is an excellent way to learn and measure the impact of specific changes and by comparing the performance of a control group with that of a variation group, you can quantify the effect of your changes on key metrics.

However, for minor changes with expected minimal impact, A/B testing may not be worth the time and resources. I remember a few times when we spent weeks running an A/B test for minor visual changes that didn't move the needle at all. Easy to guess I learned not to do these anymore and it's a good reminder that not every change warrants this level of testing. If setting up and monitoring the test is too resource-intensive, consider alternative methods and avoid A/B testing if you don't have a clear hypothesis about the expected outcomes.

How to Conduct A/B Testing

Define the hypothesis and the test objective: Have a clear hypothesis about what you expect to achieve with the change and identify the primary metric you want to test. For example, you might hypothesize that changing the call-to-action button color from blue to green will increase the click-through rate by 10% (this is known as the minimum detectable effect). To this, you should also add guardrail or risk metrics—metrics that may be impacted negatively as a result of your action.

Select the variable to test: Choose a specific element to test, such as a web page layout or a product description. Ideally, only one variable should be tested at a time to isolate its effect.

Determine the significance level (α): The significance level, often set at 0.05, represents the probability of incorrectly rejecting a hypothesis that should not be rejected (committing a Type I error). This is the threshold for determining whether the observed effect in your test is statistically significant and, in simple terms, it means there's a 5% chance of mistakenly concluding that there's a difference between the two versions when there actually isn't one. A lower alpha requires a larger sample size, leading to longer test durations, but it reduces the risk of making an incorrect conclusion.

Calculate the statistical power ($1 - \beta$): Statistical power is the probability of correctly rejecting a false null hypothesis (avoiding a Type II error). A higher power (typically 0.80 or 80%) means a higher chance of detecting a real effect when it exists. Power analysis involves considering the effect size (the magnitude of the difference you expect) and your sample size and, in layman terms, it means there's a 20% chance of concluding there is no difference between the two versions when, in fact, there is one.

Why is the Type 1 error rate set at 5% while the Type 2 error rate is set at 20%? It's because adopting a new feature without fully understanding its effects is riskier, so we need to be more stringent in detecting differences when they occur; on the other hand, continuing with the status quo is less risky, so we allow a higher probability of Type 2 errors. Reducing the Type 2 error rate means running experiments for a longer time, so there's always a trade-off.

Estimate sample size: The sample size depends on the desired significance level, statistical power, and expected effect size. Once you have these considerations in mind, you can estimate the sample size using tools like the sample size calculator from Evan Miller's website, which helps determine the number of participants needed for each group in your test.

Calculate the duration of the test: The test should run long enough to collect adequate data but not so long that external factors (like seasonal trends) could skew the results. The duration often depends on your website traffic and the conversion rates. For example, if your test requires a sample size of 10,000 users, but your website only gets 2,000 visitors a week, you would need to run the test for at least five weeks to gather enough data.

Understanding these statistical elements is quite important as I often see teams thinking their tests show promising results, only to realize they hadn't accounted for sample size correctly.

Randomize the audience: Randomly assign users to either the control group (A) or the variant group (B) to avoid selection bias and make sure the groups are comparable in terms of demographics and behavior.

Monitor the test and collect data: Once the test is live, monitor the performance of both variants and collect data on the metrics you've identified as key indicators of success.

Analyze the results: After the test concludes, analyze the data using statistical methods to determine if there is a significant difference between the two variants. Tools like t-tests or chi-square tests are commonly used for this analysis.

Make data-driven decisions: Based on the analysis, decide whether to implement the change, run additional tests, or explore other changes.

Creating Meaningful Variants

When you A/B test, create variants that are both impactful and purposeful. Ideally, you should change one specific element at a time to clearly understand its effect. For example, if you're testing a call-to-action button, you might alter its color in one variant and the text in another, but not change both simultaneously, allowing for a better measurement of how each element influences user behavior. However, in practice, A/B tests often involve more complex changes. For example, revamping a screen, changing a flow, or reordering elements can involve multiple changes in an experiment. This is acceptable if you understand that it might be challenging to identify the individual effect of each change.

To reduce risks drastically, make sure you base your decisions on clear hypotheses, which could come from user feedback, insights, or best practices in UX design. For example, if users report issues finding specific information, testing different layouts or content placements can be a good starting point. The changes you introduce should be distinct enough to potentially change user behavior, as subtle changes might not provide significant results.

Segmenting Your Audience

Randomly dividing your audience helps avoid any pre-existing biases that might influence the test outcome. However, there are times when segmentation needs to be more strategic, such as grouping users based on demographics, behavior, or purchase history and it is useful when testing features or changes aimed at a specific segment.

Be mindful of external factors that could impact the behavior of different segments, like regional differences or the types of devices used. To make sure both control and variant groups are comparable, you should perform a segmentation analysis after the first few days of the rollout. This helps to confirm that both groups have the same split on these important factors, maintaining the integrity of your test results.

Defining Success Metrics Aligned with Objectives

Clearly define what success looks like for your A/B test, aligning these metrics with your overall objectives. For example, if the goal is to increase user engagement, good metrics could include time spent on a page, interaction rates, or the number of pages viewed per session. Also, make sure that your metrics are quantifiable and directly related to the variant being tested.

When selecting the metrics, try to balance leading and lagging indicators, where leading indicators provide immediate feedback (like click rates), while lagging indicators (such as customer retention rates) offer insights into long-term impacts. I learned early on to avoid getting distracted by vanity metrics that look impressive but don't contribute meaningful insights toward your objectives. For example, a high number of page views might seem positive, but if the goal is to increase conversions, then conversion rate is a more relevant metric.

Avoid the Trial-and-Error Approach

A/B testing is most effective when it is used to test specific hypotheses grounded in solid insights. When random changes are tested instead without a good foundation, it can be challenging to interpret the results.

The lack of a clear hypothesis makes it difficult to find which factors contributed to any observed differences, reducing the reliability of the outcomes. For example, we once tested several design changes to our homepage without a clear hypothesis, and while the new design *looked* better, it didn't improve conversion rates. In contrast, a later test, where we hypothesized that simplifying the discovery process would reduce website abandonment, led to a significant 15% increase in conversions.

To avoid having dozens of failed or low impact tests, do proper user research to understand your users' needs and develop specific, data-driven hypotheses to design your tests around these hypotheses. In this way you are able to generate better insights and make informed decisions, rather than relying on a trial-and-error method.

How to Build Confidence Before A/B Testing

While A/B testing is a valuable tool for optimizing solutions, you need to build confidence on your approach before you start the implementation and test of the change. You should not use a/b testing to gain that confidence, as you would end up with a lot of failed tests (and wasted time). There are many ways to build confidence before using A/B tests.

Understanding the problem:

- User research: Surveys, interviews, and focus groups allow teams to get direct feedback from their audience. What you learn from these could give you enough understanding of the problem and how to solve it.

- Leveraging existing data: Analyzing existing data and metrics can provide insights into user behavior, helping you understand the problem more deeply. In one case, we discovered through user interviews that our assumption about a feature's low usage was incorrect— it wasn't because users didn't want it, but because it was hard to find. This insight helped us decide to promote the feature in a better way and made us scrap the A/B test we were planning to launch.

Validating the solution:

- Creating prototypes: Iterating on these based on user feedback can help teams refine their solutions before implementing them and learn if the solution has the potential to solve the problem.

- Conducting usability tests: Using prototypes can help catch issues in how users interact with a solution in real time, providing insights for refining the solution. For example, a prototype for a new onboarding process helped us identify a rather confusing step we thought was fine, that would have likely led to user drop-off and addressing this before the A/B test saved us from potential negative results.

Analyzing competitors:

- Competitor analysis: Analyzing competitors' products offers lessons on what may work and what may not work, helping you make decisions faster.

Managing Risks

You should test when the risk of deploying the feature could lead to significant issues, which can be defined as a substantial financial loss or a significant drop in key metrics. Practically, this means you need to test when you are impacting a large number of customers or high-value customers.

Be cautious when rolling out a change that comes from a strategic company decision rather than direct customer feedback. If it's a company bet, ask yourself: if the control performs better, would I stick with it? If the answer is no, then you should opt for an A/B test.

If the impact of a feature on the rest of the product is unclear, testing becomes really important.

It is also important to reiterate the need to have guardrail metrics in place during A/B tests if there is a belief that the new feature might have adverse impacts.

High Impact Projects

Your team should work on high-impact projects independently of what tools you use to test. These projects are expected to have a significant and measurable effect on higher-level metrics. Often, the impact is detectable through pre-post analysis (but this doesn't mean A/B testing should be excluded). When teams concentrate on high impact projects, their efforts contribute more materially to the company's mission.

When a launch doesn't lead to significant changes, you should critically analyze both the problem and the solution. Did you identify the wrong issue? Misjudge its size and importance? Misunderstand the cause? Solve it poorly or partially because you underestimated its complexity? You should run retrospectives to improve the understanding and decision-making of your team.

Alternatives to A/B Testing

- Pre-post analysis: Instead of comparing two groups simultaneously, you can measure key metrics before and after implementing the change and get insights into the impact without needing a control group.

- Gradual rollout: You can also gradually roll out the change to a larger audience in stages, known as a phased roll-out, allowing you to monitor the impact at each stage to ensure the effectiveness of the change.

- Regression analysis: You can perform a regression analysis to analyze the impact of a change by comparing outcomes for users just above and below a cutoff or threshold.

- Uplift modeling: Uplift modeling predicts the causal effect of a change on individual behavior by modeling the difference in outcomes between treated and untreated groups.

CASE STUDY: GADGETWORLD

An e-commerce company, GadgetWorld, identified that their checkout process had a higher-than-average abandonment rate and after conducting user research, the team believed that simplifying the checkout process could improve this metric.

Objective

Decrease the checkout abandonment rate and increase overall conversions by implementing a new checkout process.

Variants

- Variant A: The existing multistep checkout process.

- Variant B: A simplified, one-page checkout process.

Metrics and hypotheses

- Primary metric: Checkout abandonment rate.

- Secondary metrics: Conversion rate, time spent on checkout page.

- Guardrail metrics: Refund rates and contacts to avoid implementing non-transparent practices to increase the checkout rate.

- Hypothesis: Variant B will reduce the checkout abandonment rate by making the process faster and less complex.

Sample size and power analysis

Using historical data, the team calculated the required sample size to detect a 5% decrease in abandonment rate with 80% power and a significance level of 5%. Visitors were then randomly assigned to either Variant A or B, ensuring each group was representative of the overall traffic.

Duration of the test

The test was conducted over a period of six weeks to account for weekly traffic variations and collect enough data.

Results

- Variant A: 40% checkout abandonment rate.

- Variant B: 33% checkout abandonment rate.

- Statistical analysis: The difference was statistically significant ($p < 0.05$).

The results showed that the new checkout process (Variant B) significantly reduced the abandonment rate. The team also noticed an increase in overall conversions and a slight increase in the time spent on the checkout page, showing that users were more comfortable with the process.

GadgetWorld decided to implement the one-page checkout process across the website.

How to Increase Conversion Rates

In this section, we focus on synthesizing the insights and strategies discussed in Chapter 4 to effectively increase conversion rates across your product. We also address how to avoid common mistakes that many product managers make. The focus is on moving from random attempts to increase conversion rates to a methodical approach that improves both KPIs and user satisfaction.

The "Spaghetti on the Wall" Approach

The "throw spaghetti against the wall and see what sticks" approach is a known product metaphor for making random, untargeted changes to see what might work, without a clear strategy. This method is tempting when product managers feel pressure to improve performance metrics quickly. However, it's similar to flipping a coin, it may work and it may not work, and most importantly, you rarely know what part of your improvements actually worked.

Instead of addressing the root causes of issues, this approach scatters efforts across multiple aspects of the product, hoping that some change will stick and make a positive impact. Since changes are not based on a deep understanding of user behavior or data-driven insights, there is a high risk of implementing solutions that will not solve the customers' problems that are causing the drop-offs.

This way of working will also create frustrations within your company and even with your customer base. Your company will see you consuming resources and time while the metrics will barely move, while your users will be confused by frequent and random changes. Their trust in the product will erode and the overall user experience will degrade.

While the "spaghetti on the wall" method might occasionally lead to a successful result, it is not a sustainable or efficient way to optimize conversion rates. It bypasses data analysis and user research which help you build conviction and help you achieve the improvements you are looking for in a much faster and methodical way.

The Right Approach—Understand Your Data

Start by mapping out the user journey and analyzing the data to determine where users are dropping off or taking actions that do not lead to conversion. Look for patterns among users who fail to convert, as well as those who complete your flow. It's also important to segment your data to understand different user behaviors based on demographics, user types, or source of traffic. This segmentation can help you find insights into how different groups interact with your product and where they may encounter friction points.

Be mindful that, sometimes, the step where the user drops off isn't the root cause of the drop-off. For example, some customers might not convert after completing a step because they realize the product doesn't provide the service they came for. The root cause goes back to product availability or comprehension issues at the beginning of the flow. In another project, we once noticed a significant drop-off at the payment stage. After investigation, we found that users were actually unclear about the pricing structure earlier in the process and by making the pricing more transparent up-front, we saw a 20% increase in completed purchases.

You should also track and analyze user behavior over time as there may be changes in user behavior due to shifts in market trends, recent product changes, or bugs. For example, a sudden drop in conversion rates after an update might be due to some usability issues with a new feature. We once launched a new feature that, instead of increasing engagement, led to a 10% drop in conversions and after monitoring the user behavior, we found out that the feature added unnecessary steps to the conversion flow. After reducing the number of steps, conversions rebounded and even improved by 8% compared to before the feature launch.

Develop Hypotheses

Based on your data analysis, formulate hypotheses about what might be causing the drop-offs. For example, if users are abandoning their shopping carts, it may be due to a complicated checkout process or unclear pricing information.

Your hypotheses should be specific and tied directly to the insights collected from the data analysis. For example, if younger users are abandoning their carts more frequently than older users, you might hypothesize that the payment options are not aligned with younger users' preferences.

It's important that each hypothesis is actionable and testable, framing your hypotheses in a way that allows you to clearly test them through changes to the product. For example, hypothesizing that simplifying the checkout process will reduce drop-off rates gives you a clear path for testing.

Talk to Your Customers

After developing hypotheses based on your data insights, the next step is to collect user feedback to validate these hypotheses. You should engage with your customers to understand their experiences and get the insights that can either confirm your assumptions or point you in new directions.

There are many ways to engage with your customers.

Surveys are a common approach, because they allow you to collect quantitative data as well. However, make sure your survey is designed to ask pointed, clear questions that are directly tied to your hypotheses. For example, if you hypothesize that users find the checkout process too complex, your survey should include specific questions about each step of that process.

Another way to engage with your users is to schedule more in-depth interviews as they can give you qualitative insights that surveys might miss. During interviews, you should encourage users to share their thoughts freely, which can uncover deeper reasons behind their behaviors and opinions. For example, users might tell you that they find some terms confusing or that navigation buttons are not where they expect them to be.

You can also combine these methods together. For example, you could initially survey customers to get an understanding of the macro problems in your product and then use interviews to dig deeper into those problems if they happen to be too vague or need further research.

Usability testing sessions are also a good tool in a PM arsenal. During usability sessions, you observe users interacting with your product in real time to see where they find problems or have hesitation.

It's important to structure all these interactions in a way that they do not lead the user but rather allow them to provide genuine responses. This might mean setting tasks for them to complete during usability tests or framing interview questions in an open-ended way.

Ideate Solutions

Once you've validated your hypotheses through user feedback, the next step is to ideate solutions that address the identified problems effectively.

A good, collaborative way to come up with ideas is to organize brainstorming sessions with your team to generate solutions that are tailored to the specific issues your users are experiencing. You can use techniques like design thinking, which emphasizes empathy with users and encourages thinking outside the box. Incorporating user personas and jobs-to-be-done frameworks during these sessions helps everyone understand who and what problems you are solving for. I've found that bringing diverse perspectives into these sessions—like including team members from customer support or sales—can lead to better solutions.

In these sessions, no idea is too small or too far-fetched to consider. The goal is to generate a wide range of ideas that can then be refined and evaluated for feasibility.

Once a broad set of ideas has been generated, narrow them down by considering the impact on user experience, technical feasibility, alignment with business goals, and potential ROI. Prioritize ideas that are most likely to effectively solve the issues identified earlier in the process.

Prototype and Test

After ideating potential solutions, prototype and test the best ideas to see how they perform in real-world scenarios. In this way, you can build confidence that those solutions solve the identified problems without introducing new issues.

The prototypes should be functional enough to simulate the actual user interaction but don't need to be fully developed and, depending on the nature of the solution, they can go from simple mock-ups or wireframes to more interactive versions of the product.

Once the prototypes are ready, conduct testing sessions with actual users. Design the sessions to observe how users interact with the new features or changes and look for any immediate reaction, ease of use, and whether the changes actually solve the issues they're meant to solve. It's also useful to collect quantitative data during these tests and metrics like task completion rate, time on task, and user error rates can give you good evidence of a prototype's performance.

Based on the results of these tests, refine your prototypes and don't stop after the first one but make adjustments based on user feedback. You may require doing several rounds of prototyping and testing to get it right. Each iteration should bring you closer to a solution that solves the problem and also fits into the overall user journey and product ecosystem. In one project, I remember we went through seven to eight rounds of prototyping before finding the right solution. The final version exceeded our expectations and this iterative process, though time-consuming, was key to our success.

Implement and Monitor

Once a prototype has been tested and iterated on, it's time to build the solution and monitor its impact and, depending on the scope and scale of the change, you may choose to implement it in stages. For smaller changes, a full launch might be appropriate, while for more significant changes, a phased approach or A/B test can help mitigate risks. This allows you to monitor the impact incrementally and make adjustments if there are unexpected issues.

Once the solution is live, use the same metrics that you used during the testing phase to measure the solution in production.

Monitor your main KPIs closely to check whether the changes achieve your desired outcomes. This should include user engagement metrics, conversion rates, and any specific metrics related to the problem.

CASE STUDY: TECHINNOVATE

John, a product manager at TechInnovate, a mid-sized tech company specialized in productivity tools, was facing pressure to improve the conversion rates of the company's flagship product, OrganizePro. Initially, his approach was to quickly implement changes that the team thought might increase conversions, like a new onboarding tutorial, multiple layout changes to the dashboard, and simplified navigation options.

Despite the team's efforts, the results were underwhelming. Conversion rates remained stagnant, and user feedback suggested that some of the new features were actually making the product more confusing. The lack of a structured approach led to frustration within the team.

John decided to reset the team's approach. They started with a deep dive into the product's user data to identify the areas where users were dropping off.

They learned that many users were abandoning the product at the initial setup phase and the team hypothesized that the onboarding process was too complex for new users.

With this hypothesis in mind, John organized a series of user testing sessions and surveys to target the onboarding experience and the feedback confirmed that new users felt bombarded with too much information up-front.

The team brainstormed solutions to streamline the onboarding process, focusing on making it more intuitive and less cluttered and developed a prototype with a simplified step-by-step tutorial that introduced features gradually based on user actions.

This new onboarding prototype was tested with a small group of new users and the results were positive—users reported a significantly clearer understanding of how to use the product. Encouraged by these results, John led the team to implement the new onboarding process fully. They continued to monitor user feedback and conversion metrics, making small adjustments based on ongoing insights from user data.

This approach led to a 25% increase in conversion rates within the first three months after implementing the new onboarding process with the team feeling more confident in their development efforts, knowing they were based on solid data and real user feedback.

Key Product Metrics

Metrics come in multiple forms, each offering a unique view of your product's performance. From engagement metrics like session length to financial indicators like revenue growth, selecting the right metrics can make or break your product. The choice depends on your product's nature and the goals you want to achieve.

Metrics in product management can broadly be categorized into several types:

User Engagement Metrics

These metrics show how users interact with your product and common examples include daily active users, retention rate, number of returning users, session length, and page views. They help you understand user behavior, engagement, and the overall stickiness of your product. For example, in one of our mobile app projects, we focused on session length as a key metric and by analyzing it alongside user feedback, we discovered that users were spending more time on the app because they were struggling with navigation. This insight made us redesign the app to improve its usability.

Financial Metrics

Important for the business aspect of your product, these include metrics like monthly recurring revenue (MRR), lifetime value (LTV), and customer acquisition cost (CAC) and they provide insights into the financial health and profitability of your product. In a SaaS product I worked on, tracking LTV helped us find out customers who engaged with a particular feature had a 30% higher LTV than those who didn't. This insight led us to promote that feature more prominently, which in turn increased overall revenue.

Customer Satisfaction Metrics

Metrics like Net Promoter Score (NPS) and customer satisfaction score (CSAT) give you an idea of how satisfied your users are with your product. They can measure user sentiment and loyalty.

Performance Metrics

These metrics focus on the technical aspects of your product, such as load time, downtime, and error rates. They help understand if your product is reliable and performs well from a technical standpoint.

Growth Metrics

Metrics like user acquisition rate, growth rate, and market share are used to understand the growth and scalability of your product in the market.

As a product manager, you need to understand what each metric means for your product. For example, a high DAU count might mean good user engagement, but if paired with a high churn rate, it could mean that while many users are trying your product, they're not sticking around. In my experience, this dual-metric analysis is quite important. In one case, we saw a spike in DAU after a promotion, but the high churn that followed made it clear that the new users were not finding long-term value.

North Star Metric

Choosing the right metrics helps steer a product team's decision-making and prioritization, but if the wrong metrics are selected and optimized for, they can lead the team in the wrong direction. One useful approach is to identify a "north star metric"—a single, overarching metric that captures the core value your product delivers to customers. While you may track multiple metrics for different purposes, having a north star metric helps all efforts to ultimately contribute to the same goal.

To better understand the relationship between the metrics, consider using a KPI tree as the visual representation breaks down the north star metric into contributing metrics, showing how each one supports the overall objective.

Selecting the Right Metrics

If you want to choose the right metrics for your product, you need to understand what you really want to achieve and make sure the metrics you track reflect those goals. For example, if you want to increase user engagement, you should look at things like how long people spend on your app and how often they return.

You also need to think about where your product is in its life cycle; newer products might need to focus on attracting users, while older ones might focus on keeping them. It's important to understand how users are interacting with your product, so look at which features they use most and where they might be getting stuck.

Generally, choose metrics that measure performance and help you make better decisions for your product. Try to keep things simple by focusing on a few key metrics that everyone on your team understands, and make sure you measure these metrics consistently over time. In this way, you will get a clear picture of how well your product is doing and what you might need to change to make it better.

Interpreting Data for Actionable Insights

To understand what your data is telling you, look for trends over time which helps you spot any changes in how users behave or if new problems are popping up. For example, if you see more users leaving each month, it might mean they're not happy with something about your product.

Next, try to connect different types of data. For example, if you see an increase in user churn, cross-reference this with the timeline of recent feature releases or changes in customer support tickets as it can help you identify if a new feature might be causing user dissatisfaction or if there's a spike in issues after a specific update. It's a great way to see what's working and what might need a change.

Don't forget to listen to what your users are telling you directly. Combining what they say with the numbers you see can give you a much clearer picture of what's going on. It's also good to check how you stack up against others in your industry as it can show you where you're doing well and where you might need to up your game.

Regular Reviews

To confirm your metrics accurately reflect the current state of your product and market, it's important to review them regularly and to set a consistent schedule—whether weekly, bi-weekly, or monthly—based on your product's nature and market dynamics. This routine helps you monitor progress and identify emerging trends or shifts in user behavior.

During each review session, analyze any significant changes in your metrics, such as variations in user engagement, behavior shifts, or revenue fluctuations and compare these findings against your goals and industry benchmarks to understand your product's performance and market standing.

Additionally, involve your team in these reviews as different team members can offer unique insights and perspectives, helping to find areas that need a new approach.

User Acquisition Metrics

User acquisition metrics play an important role in understanding how effective you are in attracting new users, especially during and after a product launch. These metrics can give you insights into the reach, appeal, and engagement levels of your product, as well as the efficiency of your marketing efforts.

- Number of new users/sign-ups: This metric tracks the total count of users who have registered for or started using your product and it's a direct measure of the initial interest your product is generating. Trends in this metric can tell you how well your product is being received by the market; however, in my experience, many teams tend to celebrate spikes in sign-ups after a major launch, without understanding whether these new users were engaging and sticking around.

- Number of app downloads: For app-based products, download numbers are an indicator of market interest and they show how many users are installing your app. Be sure to couple this with other meaningful metrics to avoid focusing on vanity metrics.

- Conversion rate: This is the percentage of users who take the desired action (like signing up or making a transaction) out of the total number of users who started the process (like visiting your sign-up page or app store page) and a high conversion rate suggests that your flows are effective and resonate with your audience.

- Cost per acquisition (CPA): This metric tells you the cost for acquiring each new user, calculated by dividing the total acquisition expenses by the number of new users and it's good for understanding the financial efficiency of your marketing campaigns. I've seen product managers underestimate the importance of optimizing CPA. In one case, by changing focus to more cost-effective channels, one of my teams was able to lower their CPA by more than 60%, which allowed for more sustainable growth over time.

- User acquisition rate: This measures the speed at which new users are being added and it's calculated by comparing the number of new users within a specific period to the total user base at the start of that period.

- Channel-specific acquisition data: With this metric, you can learn which marketing channel is best at driving user sign-ups and can help you understand where to focus your marketing efforts.

Revenue Metrics

Revenue metrics offer a view of a product's financial performance and can help you understand the economic impact of the product.

- Total sales revenue generated: This metric shows the total income from product sales giving you insights into sales trends. It's a straightforward indicator of the product's market performance and helps in evaluating how effective your sales strategies are.

- Average revenue per user (ARPU): ARPU is the revenue divided by the number of users or customers and it shows how much revenue each user contributed on average. A higher ARPU suggests that users find high value in the product, which is especially significant for products with recurring revenue models like subscriptions.

- Revenue growth rate: This metric tracks the rate at which revenue grows over a period and while it indicates how well your product is performing financially, it should be compared with overall market growth to understand market penetration. For instance, if your revenue grows by 50% but the market grows by 70%, your market share has actually decreased.

- Lifetime value (LTV) of a customer: LTV estimates the total revenue a customer will generate over their entire relationship with the product. It's a measure of long-term customer value and it's useful to understand the profitability of customer acquisition and retention.

- Profit margin: Profit margin, calculated as revenue minus costs divided by revenue, shows the efficiency of the product in generating profit and it is important for assessing the financial health and sustainability of the product.

Engagement and Retention Metrics

Engagement metrics help evaluate how users interact with your product and they offer insights into user behavior, showing areas where the product is succeeding in capturing user interest and areas that may require some changes.

- Daily/Monthly active users (DAU/MAU): These metrics track the number of unique users who engage with the product daily or monthly. A high DAU/MAU ratio shows strong user engagement and the choice between daily or monthly metrics depends on the use case frequency. For example, measure daily engagement for a social media platform like Facebook, while a weekly engagement metric might be more relevant for a gym app.

- Session duration: This metric measures the average amount of time users spend on your product during each visit. Longer session durations can indicate higher user engagement, suggesting that users find the content or features valuable. However, it could also mean that the user journey is not intuitive, causing users to spend more time looking for what they need.

- User interaction rate: Understanding how users interact with specific features of your product can tell you what's working well and what isn't. High interaction rates can show a specific feature's popularity, while low interaction rates may highlight the areas that need improvement.

- Bounce Rate: Bounce rate measures the percentage of visitors who leave after viewing only one page or section. A lower bounce rate may mean users are finding what they're looking for and are inclined to explore more.

- Retention rate: This metric measures the percentage of users who return to the product over a specific period. High retention rates are indicative of a product that continues to meet user needs over time, encouraging them to come back.

- Churn rate: Churn rate measures the percentage of users who stop using the product and keeping it low is fundamental for the overall product success.

Customer Satisfaction Metrics

Customer satisfaction metrics show how users perceive and value your product, reflecting their satisfaction and overall experience.

- Net promoter score (NPS): NPS is a widely used metric that measures customer loyalty and satisfaction and it's calculated based on responses to the question: "On a scale of 0-10, how likely are you to recommend our product to a friend or colleague?" Scores of 9–10 are considered "Promoters," 7–8 are "Passives," and 0–6 are "Detractors." NPS is the percentage of promoters minus the percentage of detractors and provides a clear indication of overall customer sentiment toward the product.

- Customer satisfaction score (CSAT): This metric is directly derived from customer feedback, usually collected through surveys asking customers to rate their satisfaction with the product. Typically measured on a scale (like 1–5 or 1–10), the CSAT score gives a quick snapshot of how satisfied customers are with your product at a given moment.

- Customer reviews and ratings: Online reviews and ratings, whether on your product page, app stores, or third-party review sites, are valuable sources of customer satisfaction data.

- Customer effort score (CES): CES measures the ease of user experience with your product and it's based on asking customers how much effort they had to put in to use the product or resolve an issue. Lower effort scores are generally indicative of a more user-friendly and satisfying product experience. Studies, such as those by Harvard Business Review, have shown that reducing customers' effort can significantly increase their loyalty and decrease churn rates.

- Referral rates: The rate at which existing customers refer new users to your product can also be a strong indicator of customer satisfaction. Higher referral rates often correlate with higher overall customer satisfaction.

Market Penetration Metrics

Market penetration metrics provide insights into a product's reach and presence in its target market and help determine how well the product competes in its space and its success in capturing a share of the market.

- Market share percentage: This metric indicates the product's share of the total market sales. Calculated by dividing the product's sales by the total market sales, an increasing market share suggests a growing acceptance and dominance of your product among consumers.

- Penetration rate: This measures the extent to which a product has been adopted compared to the total potential market. It's done by dividing the number of actual customers by the total potential customers, offering an idea of how much of the market is using the product.

- Brand recognition: Measuring brand awareness through surveys and market research can inform how recognizable and memorable the brand is among the target audience.

- Comparative market share: Comparing your market share with competitors offers a perspective on the product's competitive standing and it helps identify opportunities to increase market share. For example, if a competitor has a higher share in a particular demographic or region, it could indicate an opportunity to target those areas with marketing strategies or product changes.

CHAPTER 5

Go-to-Market and Product Launch

This chapter will guide you through the journey of launching and sustaining a product in the marketplace. In this chapter, we explore go-to-market strategies and product launch dynamics and you'll learn how to leverage market forces and align your product with the needs and desires of your audience to guarantee a successful product launch.

Topics in this chapter:

1. **Developing a Strong Go-to-Market Strategy:** Learn how to create a GTM strategy that aligns with your product goals and target market, setting the stage for a successful launch.

2. **Maximizing Product Launch Impact:** Discover strategies to make your product launch memorable, generating buzz and driving user adoption.

Developing a Strong Go-to-Market Strategy

Launching a product into the market with a robust go-to-market strategy is all about creating a plan that makes your product resonate with your audience to drive adoption.

© Michele Galli 2025
M. Galli, *Navigating the Product Galaxy*, https://doi.org/10.1007/979-8-8688-1148-7_5

The GTM strategy is an effort that primarily involves the marketing team as they are responsible for understanding the product, the market, and the target audience to create campaigns that drive product adoption. The PM plays a supporting role (but could also be the driving force depending on the size and structure of the organization) by providing insights about the product and helping align with the overall vision. In my experience, the most successful launches happen when the PM and marketing team work very closely together.

The PM should provide information about the product's features, benefits, and differentiators, and help the marketing team create the right messaging and positioning. Together, they work to have a product launch that resonates with the target market.

Understanding Your Audience

The first step of any successful GTM is market research, as the team should analyze industry trends, understand the competitive landscape, and identify potential gaps where the product can fit. You can use surveys, interviews, focus groups, and analysis of secondary data, to get an understanding of the market dynamics.

Alongside market analysis, you should break down your potential customers into groups based on shared characteristics like demographics, behaviors, or needs to enable targeted strategies as each group may require a different approach.

When you do so, you will also be able to create buyer personas, which are semi-fictional representations of your ideal customers, created based on research and data. They include demographics, behavior patterns, motivations, and goals, helping you grasp the needs, challenges, and decision-making processes of your audience.

You should then go deeper into the specific problems, challenges, and needs of your potential customers, what pain points does your product address? How does it improve your customers' lives or work? The answers to these questions help you position your product as a solution to your customers' needs and create a message that resonates with them.

Create Your Value Proposition

Your value proposition communicates the essential message of your product to the market and distills its essence into a clear, short statement that articulates how it solves your customers' problems, delivers specific benefits, and stands out from the competition.

You should try to focus on the core benefits your product offers, identifying the unique elements that set it apart in the marketplace, whether it's saving time, reducing costs, or improving efficiency or quality.

Your understanding of the target audience guides you in framing your message in a way that aligns with your customers' needs and it should clearly communicate what your product does, who it is for, and why it is beneficial, avoiding technical language that could confuse potential customers. The goal is to make your product's value immediately clear to anyone encountering it.

Your value proposition should also highlight what sets your product apart from others, this might be a unique feature, better technology, exceptional customer service, or a more attractive price point to capture the attention of potential customers and distinguish your product in a market.

Emotional Connection

Creating an emotional connection with your audience through your product messaging is a powerful aspect of your value proposition and it helps you create a bond with your audience by resonating with their feelings, values, and aspirations. I've observed that products that successfully tap into their users' emotions tend to have higher loyalty and engagement.

To do so, you'll need to understand the emotional drivers of your target audience, what are their hopes, fears, and desires? How can your product play a role in their lives beyond its functional use? For example, if your product is a productivity app, the functional benefit might be organizing tasks efficiently, but the emotional appeal could be the sense of calm and control it brings to a user's chaotic work life.

Storytelling is a powerful tool in building an emotional connection as narratives that show relatable situations or challenges and illustrate how your product can positively impact these scenarios can be quite effective. The stories should be authentic and align with your brand's values, creating a narrative that your audience can see themselves in.

The tone of your messaging also plays an important role in creating an emotional bond, whether it's friendly, inspirational, reassuring, or empowering, the tone should reflect the emotions you want to evoke in your audience. You should then be consistent in this tone across all your marketing materials to reinforce the emotional message.

Engaging with your audience on a personal level can also improve the emotional connection as direct engagement makes customers feel heard and valued, improving their emotional connection with your brand. However, your messaging should be genuine and not seen as manipulative as authenticity in your messaging builds trust and credibility with your audience. In my experience, when a brand is authentic with its customers, it often leads to stronger, long-term relationships with them.

Choosing the Right Channels

Deciding on the most effective channels to reach your audience is another important aspect of your GTM strategy. The channels could be a mix of digital marketing, social media, content marketing, or even traditional advertising, depending on where your target audience is most active and the goal is to use them to communicate your value proposition to your audience. I've seen teams struggle when they try to be everywhere at once, so prioritize carefully as the most effective GTM strategies are those that focus on a few key channels where the target audience is most engaged.

Aligning Product and Market Readiness

The timing of your product launch should ideally leverage favorable market trends, avoid clashing with major competitive releases, and consider factors like seasonal demand. A well-timed launch can significantly improve the product's market reception, whereas poor timing might lead to an underwhelming response. Your promotional efforts should be geared up to create a buzz around the product launch by rolling out advertising campaigns, public relations efforts, social media strategies, and content marketing initiatives.

You should also make sure your team is ready, from product development to marketing, sales, and customer support, every team should be aligned and prepared for the launch. Organize briefing sessions about the product's features, its value proposition, and the specific roles and expectations for each department in the launch process and make sure to also prepare your customer support team for the post-launch as they should be ready to handle customer questions. In my experience, the difference between a good launch and a chaotic one often comes down to how well-prepared the customer support team is.

Cross-functional Collaboration

A successful GTM strategy requires collaboration across multiple teams within your organization as each team contributes its unique strengths and knowledge to address the challenges of bringing a new product to market.

The product development team, with their understanding of the product's capabilities, informs other departments about the technical aspects and potential use cases of the product. Marketing creates the narrative around the product and develops strategies to reach the target audience effectively to create market demand for the product. Sales teams and customer support teams provide feedback from customers, often highlighting additional features that could improve the product's market fit.

For a product launch to be successful, these teams must work in unison, guided by a shared understanding of the product's goals and market strategy, while leadership encourages open communication, facilitating the sharing of resources and information across departments so that all teams are aligned with the product's goals.

Iterative Approach

Be prepared to iterate and adapt your GTM strategy, as once you start collecting data and feedback post-launch, you will need to make adjustments. You should launch the product in phases or with a set of core features, then gradually refining and expanding based on user feedback and market response to allow for more agility as opposed to trying to perfect every aspect of the product before launch. Real-world user interactions will inevitably provide insights that are not always foreseeable in the development phase.

By releasing a minimum viable product or a beta version first, you can collect data on user behavior, preferences, and pain points, which then inform the next iterations.

GO-TO-MARKET STRATEGY TEMPLATE

1. **Executive summary**

   Brief overview of the product and the goals of the go-to-market strategy

2. **Market analysis**

   Market size and growth: Overview of the market size, growth rate, and trends

Target market: Description of the target market, including geographic, demographic, and psychographic details

Competitive analysis: Assessment of key competitors, their strengths, weaknesses, and market positioning

3. **Customer segmentation and personas**

   Customer segments: Distinct customer segments within the target market

   Customer personas: Detailed descriptions of customer personas, including their needs, challenges, behaviors, and motivations

4. **Value proposition and product positioning**

   Unique Selling Proposition: Clear statement of what makes the product unique and valuable to customers

   Positioning statement: How the product is positioned in the market relative to competitors

5. **Marketing and sales strategy**

   Marketing goals: Specific marketing objectives aligned with the overall strategy

   Marketing channels: Key marketing channels to reach the target audience (e.g., social media, email marketing, content marketing)

   Sales strategy: Outline of the sales approach, including sales channels and key sales activities

6. **Distribution channels**

   Description of how the product will be distributed to customers (e.g., online, retail, direct sales)

7. **Pricing strategy**

Overview of pricing strategy, including pricing model and justification

8. **Launch plan**

Launch timeline: Key milestones and timeline for the product launch

Promotional activities: Specific marketing and promotional activities planned for the launch

9. **Key metrics and success criteria**

KPIs to measure the success of the GTM strategy

10. **Risk management**

Potential risks and challenges associated with the GTM strategy and mitigation plans

11. **Post-launch plan**

Outline of post-launch activities, including customer feedback collection, product updates, and ongoing marketing efforts

---

MARKETING CHANNEL DECISION MATRIX

A matrix to evaluate and select the most effective marketing channels for your product. Consider factors like channel reach, audience fit, cost, and conversion potential.

To illustrate a marketing channel decision matrix, let's consider a hypothetical scenario for a product (Table 5-1). In this matrix, we'll evaluate various marketing channels based on three key factors:

- Reach (the potential audience size)

- Audience Fit (how well the channel aligns with the target audience)

- Cost Efficiency (the cost-effectiveness of the channel)

These factors are rated on a scale of 1 to 10.

Here's a description of how the matrix might look:

Table 5-1. *Marketing channel decision matrix example*

Marketing Channel	Reach (1–10)	Audience Fit (1–10)	Cost Efficiency (1–10)
Social Media	8	9	7
Email Marketing	5	6	8
Content Marketing	7	8	6
Traditional Advertising	6	4	3

- Social media scores high on reach and audience fit, making it ideal for targeting a broad and relevant audience efficiently.

- Email marketing is highly cost-efficient and moderately effective in terms of reach and audience fit, useful for targeted communication.

- Content marketing offers a good balance of reach and audience fit but is less cost-efficient compared to other channels.

- Traditional advertising has moderate reach and low audience fit and cost efficiency, making it less ideal for targeted or budget-conscious campaigns.

TEMPLATES TO IMPROVE YOUR MESSAGING

Message mapping template

Organize and refine your product messaging and include sections for defining the target audience, key message points, supporting details, and the channels for message delivery. For example, a section of the template could be dedicated to outlining the primary benefit of the product, followed by bullet points of supporting features or testimonials.

Product/Service name:

[Insert Product/Service]

Target audience:

[Define the primary audience for the product, including demographic and psychographic details]

Key message points:

[Main Benefit #1]: [Supporting Detail or Example]

[Main Benefit #2]: [Supporting Detail or Example]

[Main Benefit #3]: [Supporting Detail or Example]

Unique selling proposition:

[What makes your product/service unique in the market?]

Emotional appeal:

[What emotions do you want to evoke in your audience? For example, Security, Happiness, Convenience]

Proof points and testimonials:

[Customer Testimonial #1]

[Data Point or Statistic #1]

[Customer Testimonial #2]

[Data Point or Statistic #2]

Objection handling:

[Common Objection #1]: [Counterargument or Reassurance]

[Common Objection #2]: [Counterargument or Reassurance]

Call to action:

[What do you want the audience to do after receiving the message? For example, visit a website, make a purchase, sign up]

Communication channels:

[Channel #1]: [Specific adaptation of the message for this channel]

[Channel #2]: [Specific adaptation of the message for this channel]

[Channel #3]: [Specific adaptation of the message for this channel]

Brand voice and style notes:

[Notes on tone, language style, and brand personality to be reflected in the messaging]

AIDA model technique

Use the AIDA (Attention, Interest, Desire, Action) model to structure your messaging and grab the audience's attention with a compelling statement or question, build interest with specific details about your product, create desire by highlighting the benefits, and end with a call to action.

For example, a social media ad campaign could first showcase an eye-catching image of the product (Attention), describe its unique features (Interest), explain how it makes the user's life better (Desire), and finish with a prompt to purchase or learn more (Action).

Here's an example of how it can be applied in a marketing campaign for a hypothetical product, let's say a new eco-friendly coffee cup called "GreenCup."

Attention: Launch the campaign with an eye-catching image of the GreenCup on social media, with a bold question like, "Is your morning coffee harming the planet?" to grab the attention of environmentally conscious coffee drinkers.

Interest: Once you have the audience's attention, provide interesting facts that keep them engaged. For GreenCup, you could follow up with, "Every year, billions of disposable cups end up in landfills. GreenCup offers a stylish, sustainable alternative." Here, you're building interest by highlighting the problem and introducing GreenCup as a solution.

Desire: Create a desire for the product by focusing on its benefits and how it aligns with the customer's values. You might say, "GreenCup isn't just good for the environment; it's designed for the perfect coffee experience. With GreenCup you're joining a movement to save our planet, one cup at a time" to connect the product with the audience's desire to make positive environmental choices.

Action: Finally, encourage the audience to take a specific action. This could be, "Join the green movement today. Grab your own GreenCup from our website and enjoy a special 20% launch discount!" to give interested individuals a direct way to purchase the product and participate in the environmental cause.

Emotional appeal framework

Implement a framework for creating messages with emotional appeal, identify common emotions to target, such as happiness, security, or belonging, and align your product benefits with these emotions. For example, if your product is a security system, your messaging could focus on the peace of mind and sense of security it provides to families.

Here's an example of how this framework can be applied, using a hypothetical new fitness app called "FitJourney" as the product.

Identify the target emotions: For FitJourney, the target emotions might be inspiration, motivation, and a sense of achievement which resonate with people looking to improve their fitness and health.

Create the message:

Inspiration: Use stories or testimonials of real people who have transformed their lives using FitJourney. For example, a video featuring a user who went from being sedentary to running their first 5K, talking about how FitJourney inspired and guided them through their journey.

Motivation: Highlight motivational aspects of the app through messages like, "Every step counts, and FitJourney is here to cheer you on your path to fitness. Start your journey today, and see where it takes you!"

Achievement: Celebrate milestones and achievements within the app and showcase features like milestone badges or success stories, and use messages that highlight the sense of achievement users will feel. For example, "With FitJourney, every milestone is a celebration of your progress. Watch yourself achieve goals you never thought possible!"

Visual and audio elements:

Use energetic visuals in your marketing materials that evoke a sense of action and include uplifting music in advertisements to reinforce the emotional appeal.

Authenticity in messaging:

Make sure that the emotional appeal in your messaging is genuine and aligns with the real experiences of your users as authenticity is key to making an emotional connection and building trust with your audience.

Competitive positioning matrix

Develop a competitive positioning matrix to visually map out where your product stands in relation to competitors on key attributes and identify areas for differentiation in your messaging.

For example, plot competitors on a graph based on price and quality, and identify where your product fits in this spectrum. Imagine we have a product and three competitors in the market (Table 5-2). The two dimensions we will use for comparison are Quality (how well the product meets customer needs) and Price (affordability or value for money). These are rated on a scale of 1 to 10, where a higher score indicates better quality or more affordability.

Here's how the matrix might look:

Table 5-2. *Competitive positioning matrix*

Product	Quality (1–10)	Price (1–10)
Our Product	8	7
Competitor A	6	5
Competitor B	7	9
Competitor C	5	6

In this matrix:

- "Our Product" has high quality and is moderately priced.

- "Competitor A" has lower quality and is less affordable.

- "Competitor B" has good quality and is very affordable.

- "Competitor C" has the lowest quality and is less affordable.

This matrix can be visualized on a graph with Quality on the x-axis and Price on the y-axis. Each product is a point on this graph. The positioning of each point helps in understanding how products compare against each other and can guide the decisions about how to position our product in the market, such as focusing on its high quality or considering a price adjustment to become more competitive.

Customer testimonials

Collect customer testimonials that specifically address how your product has made a difference and use these testimonials in your messaging to add authenticity. For example, video testimonials or written case studies can be powerful in demonstrating real-life benefits of your product.

Testimonial example: Easy to Use

Customer: Michael D.

Location: Seattle, Washington

Quote: "*I'm not particularly tech-savvy, but EcoTherm was incredibly easy to set up and use. The app is intuitive, and I love being able to control my home temperature from anywhere.*"

Brand voice guidelines

Create a document outlining your brand voice guidelines, including the tone, language, and style that should be used in all communications to guarantee consistency. For example, if your brand voice is friendly and approachable, provide examples of how this tone should be reflected in different types of messaging. For example:

Brand overview:

GreenEarth Outdoors provides high-quality, sustainable outdoor gear for adventurous and environmentally conscious consumers. Our mission is to inspire and equip individuals to enjoy the outdoors responsibly.

Brand personality:

- Adventurous: We embody the spirit of adventure in all our communications.

- Inspirational: Our messaging motivates and encourages an active, outdoor lifestyle.

- Environmentally conscious: We are committed to sustainability and express this commitment in our language.

- Friendly and approachable: Our tone is warm, inviting, and inclusive.

Tone of voice:

- Optimistic: We focus on the joy and fulfillment that comes from outdoor adventures and environmental stewardship.

- Conversational: Our language is simple, clear, and free of jargon. We speak to our customers as knowledgeable friends.

- Inspiring: We aim to inspire action toward outdoor adventures and environmental consciousness.

- Respectful: We communicate with a deep respect for nature and our community.

Language style:

- Use active voice: Keep sentences engaging and direct.

- Be descriptive but concise: Use vivid imagery to describe our products and the outdoor experience, but avoid overcomplicating messages.

- Inclusive language: Make sure that our content is accessible and inclusive to all, regardless of background or experience level in outdoor activities.

- Sustainability-focused terminology: Use terms that highlight our commitment to sustainability, like "eco-friendly," "sustainable," "biodegradable," etc.

Brand voice in action:

- Product description: "Experience the wild in comfort and style with our EcoTrek boots—sustainably created to last through every adventure."

- Social media post: "There's nothing like the tranquility of a forest at dawn. What's your favorite nature spot to find peace? 🌿 ☼

- Customer service communication: "Hi there! We're thrilled you're joining the GreenEarth family. If you have any questions about your gear, we're here to help."

Visual content:

- Imagery: Use vibrant, high-quality images that reflect the beauty of the natural world and the joy of outdoor activities.

- Brand colors and fonts: Adhere to our brand color palette and fonts for consistency in visual identity.

Maximizing Product Launch Impact

If you want to capture the market's attention and set the stage for the product's future success, you will have to maximize the impact of your product launch. A great launch can create a strong foundation for your sales.

Here are some good strategies to maximize the impact of your launch.

Launch Planning

As for everything, you will need a plan to make sure your launch goes as expected. Set a timeline to mark the milestones, like finalizing the product and kicking off marketing campaigns and to go through the life cycle of the launch, from the initial buzz to post-launch.

Next, set the goals for the launch which will range from brand awareness metrics to sales figures. Then, create the marketing and promotion strategy, which should include each medium you plan to use, whether it's social media, email, or public relations, telling a consistent story of your product. The last step of the plan is to make sure you synchronize your launch with your customer-facing teams so they know the story your product should tell.

Pre-launch

When you are able to build anticipation and excitement among your audience, you will have good chances to have a successful launch for your product. One way to do it is by using teasers and sneak peeks of your product through social media posts, short teaser videos, or cryptic messages that hint at the product's benefits without giving away too much to get people talking about what's coming.

Another way marketing teams create buzz is by using influencers and industry experts to extend your reach and add credibility to your product. They can share their experiences or expectations of your product in a way that resonates with their followers, creating a more authentic anticipation.

Whatever technique you use, social media is usually the best place to start conversations around your product. For example, you can create interactive campaigns, such as hashtags, contests, or Q&A sessions, that encourage the audience to participate with the goal to involve your audience in the pre-launch phase, making them feel part of the product journey and building a community around your launch.

You can also incorporate email campaigns to directly engage with your existing customer base and offer, for example, early access to encourage a sense of exclusivity and, where possible, create interactive content or demos to give a taste of what's to come like a virtual product tour or an interactive feature on your website.

Last but not least, use public relations and media to get your product featured in industry news, popular blogs, or other media outlets.

Leveraging Multiple Channels

Identify which channels are most effective for reaching your audience like social media, email marketing, and online advertising, as well as more traditional channels such as print media, television, or radio ads. The key is to understand where your audience spends their time and how they consume information.

Once you've identified these channels, develop a strategy that tailors your message to the strengths and audience of each channel while maintaining a consistent message. For example, social media can be used for more engaging content, like live Q&A sessions, behind-the-scenes looks, or user-generated content while email marketing, on the other hand, might be better for in-depth information or special offers.

Make sure you plan your content calendar, as timing can make the difference, depending on the channel you use. For example, you can tease a major announcement on social media, detail it in an email campaign, and then explore it in a blog post.

Content should be adapted to fit the format and style of each channel while reinforcing the same key messages. On Instagram, you might use nice visuals and short, impactful messages, while on your website you may use a more detailed product overview.

In addition to your owned channels, consider partnerships with influencers, brand ambassadors, or business partners to amplify your message through their networks.

Event-Led Launch

An event-led launch uses the power of a focused, engaging event to create a significant impact at the introduction of your product and it should align with the nature of your product and the preferences of your target audience. For example, for a tech product you may want to organize a high-energy, tech-savvy launch event or an interactive virtual reality experience while for a lifestyle brand you might opt for a more intimate, experiential event that allows attendees to physically interact with the product.

The event should tell a story about the brand and the journey to this point, from the visuals to the activities available to attendees as I've found that the right event can have quite an impact on your launch. For example, we once organized an event for the launch of a smart home app where we invited early adopters and investors to a rented building in London, fully equipped with connected smart devices. Attendees were able to interact with the app in a real-world environment, controlling everything from lighting to security.

To promote the event, use your marketing channels—social media, email, public relations—to tease details and generate excitement. The content and activities at the event should be engaging and could be beneficial to have key members of your team, such as product developers or executives, available to interact with the attendees.

The follow-up post-event is as important as the event itself, you could send thank-you notes to attendees, share the event highlights and media coverage, and continue the conversation started at the event through your marketing channels with the aim to maintain the momentum generated by the event and to use it to push your product further into the market.

Post-Launch Feedback

After you launch your product, make sure to monitor social media as customers often turn to these platforms to express their opinions, making them valuable sources of unfiltered feedback. It's a good practice to regularly check platforms like Twitter, Facebook, Instagram, and LinkedIn, as well as review sites like Amazon, Yelp, or industry-specific forums to capture what customers are saying about your product in these spaces.

You can also use tools like Hootsuite, Sprout Social, or Google Alerts to track mentions of your product across the web as they offer the ability to analyze trends and sentiments over time which help in identifying both positive feedback and addressing any negative comments.

However, It's not enough to just listen; responding to customer feedback on these platforms is also important, from thanking customers for positive reviews to addressing complaints as responding to feedback shows that your company values customer input and is committed to improving the customer experience.

Social media and online reviews can also provide insights into how your product is being used in real life, which may differ from how it was originally intended. Another aspect to consider is the impact of influencers and opinion leaders in your industry as they can change the public perception; you should monitor their opinions and reviews to understand how your product is being received by them.

CHAPTER 6

Team Leadership, Collaboration, and Ethical Considerations

This chapter helps you navigate the challenges of team leadership, build a culture of collaboration, and uphold the ethical standards that are the foundation of every great leader. Here, you'll learn how to create a team environment that thrives on trust, where transparent communication helps you navigate misunderstandings and move your team forward together. We will explore how you can embrace diversity to bring each unique perspective and how to maintain peace and harmony through conflict resolution. Finally, we will look at how to develop future leaders to ensure your legacy continues to guide others long after your journey is over.

While this chapter focuses on leadership within the context of product management, many of the principles discussed here may apply to other roles of responsibility as well, including CEOs, CTOs, and CFOs. Effective leadership, ethical decision-making, and conflict resolution are fundamental skills for anyone in a leadership position and while we explore these principles through the lens of a product manager, they are valuable for all leaders, as understanding and applying these principles can improve your ability to lead, inspire, and navigate the complex challenges that come with any leadership role.

© Michele Galli 2025
M. Galli, *Navigating the Product Galaxy*, https://doi.org/10.1007/979-8-8688-1148-7_6

Topics in this chapter: ·

1. **Building a Culture of Trust and Transparency:** Discover how to create an environment where team members feel valued and empowered to share their ideas.

2. **Effective Communication Strategies:** Learn how to master clear, consistent communication to make sure your team remains aligned, motivated, and efficient.

3. **Diversity and Inclusivity in Team Building:** Understand the importance of building a diverse team and how to embrace inclusivity for better problem-solving.

4. **Ethical Decision-Making:** Navigate the complexities of ethical dilemmas in product management and learn how to make decisions that align with your organization's values.

5. **Conflict Resolution and Consensus Building:** Gain insights into resolving conflicts constructively and building consensus within your team, crucial for maintaining a healthy and productive work environment.

6. **Leadership Development:** Discover the importance of developing future leaders within your team and how to plan for succession to guarantee continued success.

Building a Culture of Trust and Transparency

Creating a culture of trust within a product team guarantees that every team member is heard and valued. This section will guide you through how to build trust and transparency to create an efficient team.

Lead by Example

When you, as a product manager, share your thought processes and challenges openly, it creates an environment of openness as your integrity and ethical behavior set a standard for the team. I've found that when I openly discuss the reasoning behind my decisions, it helps build trust and also empowers my team to contribute more meaningfully.

When you are open to feedback and value your team's perspectives, you are nurturing a collaborative environment, and when you view failures as opportunities for growth, you are setting a powerful example as it shows your team that challenges are steps toward success. It also shows that being in a state of constant evolution is what you expect.

Remember to seek and collect feedback from your team; bigger the engagement from your team, deeper the sense of ownership and investment from them. You can also set regular check-ins to connect with each team member, understand their progress, and address any challenges they might be facing. These are also an opportunity to share constructive feedback to help the team learn, but it's important to approach feedback with a mindset of growth, focusing on solutions and opportunities for development.

Transparency in Decision-Making

If you want to create a sense of transparency within your team, you will need to openly share the "whys" behind your decisions and walk your team through the thought process that led to a particular decision, whether it's about strategy, design, or process changes. In this way it will be much easier for your team to see the bigger picture and their role in it.

By including the team in the decision-making process, seeking their input, and discussing the reasoning behind final decisions, you encourage an environment of ownership and help the team to see how their work and the broader goals of the project are connected. It also helps demystify the process, reducing uncertainties, and aligning the team toward common objectives.

Encourage and Act on Feedback

When you receive feedback, acknowledge it and create a plan for addressing it. Prioritize the feedback and incorporate it into your team's processes where applicable and follow up on the actions taken based on feedback to communicate back to the team how their input has been used and the impact it has made.

Additionally, train the team on effective ways to give and receive feedback to improve the quality of the feedback and always see feedback as a positive and integral part of personal and professional growth. Recognizing and rewarding team members who actively engage in the feedback process can encourage a more open and constructive feedback environment.

Building Psychological Safety

Your team members should feel safe to take risks, voice their opinions, and be vulnerable without fear of negative repercussions. To create this kind of environment, you should lead with empathy, actively listening to team members and validating their experiences and feelings.

Encourage honest conversations about mistakes and learning opportunities, and make it clear that these are part of the growth process. Recognize and celebrate the efforts and contributions of team members, showing that their input is valued and appreciated.

Effective Communication Strategies

To make sure your team is aligned, you will need to master the art of clear communication, including what you communicate, how you communicate, and when you communicate. You will need different channels for different types of information, like project updates, feedback, or brainstorming sessions to tailor your communication style to your audience; I've learned that what works for one team member may not necessarily work for another.

For example, use email for formal communications, instant messaging for quick updates or questions, and dedicated project management tools for tracking progress. In my experience, understanding the strengths and limitations of each medium helps ensure that the right message is delivered in the most effective way.

Tailoring your communication style to your audience is equally important. Recognize that team members have different preferences and adapt accordingly as some may respond better to direct emails, while others might prefer detailed discussions in meetings. Being flexible and responsive to these preferences shows respect for individual working styles and can significantly improve collaboration.

Make sure you balance formal and informal communication with your team. While formal communications help clarity and record-keeping, informal interactions, such as casual conversations or team lunches, can break down barriers and encourage a more open and collaborative environment.

Active Listening

Active listening is an art that requires practice and dedication and it's about fully engaging with the speaker, understanding their message, and responding thoughtfully.

To develop this skill, you should practice full attention during conversations by putting aside distractions and focusing solely on the speaker, showing them through your body language and eye contact that you are fully engaged. Avoid the common trap of thinking about how you will respond while the other person is speaking—focus on understanding their message deeply, including their motives and intentions. In my experience, this level of engagement encourages team members to share their thoughts more openly, leading to better discussions.

Encourage an environment where team members feel comfortable sharing their thoughts without fear of interruption or judgment. Ask open-ended questions to invite deeper insights and show the speaker that you're interested in their perspective.

Reflective listening is another powerful tool. By paraphrasing or summarizing what has been said, you demonstrate your understanding which as a result clarifies the message and builds trust between you and the speaker.

Inclusivity in Communication

Every team member, regardless of their background or communication style, should feel heard and understood.

Recognize and respect cultural, linguistic, and individual differences as some team members might prefer direct communication, while others may communicate more subtly.

Adapt your communication style to be clear and accessible to all team members by simplifying language, avoiding jargon, or providing translations for non-native speakers and be mindful of non-verbal communication differences, as gestures and expressions can vary significantly across cultures. The objective is to create a safe space where everyone feels comfortable voicing their opinions through regular check-ins, anonymous feedback systems, or brainstorming sessions where everyone is encouraged to contribute. As a leader, the role of a PM is not only to be mindful of their own communication style but also to provide feedback to team members who may unintentionally prevent others from feeling safe.

Digital Communication

It's important to establish clear guidelines or "netiquette" for digital communication by setting expectations for response times, appropriate use of different communication platforms, and guidelines for online meetings, such as muting when not speaking or using video when possible.

Another key aspect is ensuring that digital communication tools are accessible to all team members by considering time zone differences for team members in different locations and making sure that all necessary information is readily accessible for future reference.

Diversity and Inclusivity in Team Building

Embracing diversity requires actively developing an environment where this diversity translates into effective problem-solving. I strongly believe that when diversity is truly embraced, it enriches team dynamics and leads to more innovative solutions.

Recruitment and Hiring

Expand your search to include diverse talent pools and engage with communities, forums, and networks that are often underrepresented in the industry.

In the job descriptions, use a language that is neutral and welcoming to all candidates and highlight your company's commitment to diversity. Not only is this the right thing to do but I've seen many times how well candidates respond when they see a clear commitment to diversity in job postings, which can attract a broader range of applicants.

In interviews, you can make the process fairer by standardizing the questions and using a diverse panel in the selection process. This helps ensure that all candidates are evaluated on an equal footing, which I've found leads to more equitable hiring outcomes. It's important that each candidate is evaluated on the same criteria to level the playing field for all.

Look beyond traditional markers of success, such as prestigious educational backgrounds or previous big-name employers, to find candidates with diverse experiences, viewpoints, and fresh perspectives.

Onboarding is the final piece of the puzzle, where you should create a welcoming and inclusive environment like mentorship programs and diversity training to make sure new hires feel supported and integrated into the team. It's also important to clearly signpost where new hires with specific needs can request appropriate support, making sure everyone has the resources they need to thrive.

Training and Development

Invest in regular diversity and inclusivity training by integrating these concepts into the standard onboarding process, so that new team members start their journey with a clear understanding of the company's commitment to these values. These training programs should cover a spectrum of topics, including understanding unconscious biases, appreciating cultural differences, and learning effective communication across diverse groups.

Inclusive Leadership

As a leader, set the tone by being inclusive in your actions and decisions and be mindful of language, understand cultural sensitivities, and ensure all team members have equal opportunities to contribute and advance.

This leadership style requires a deep commitment to understanding and appreciating the diverse backgrounds and perspectives of team members by actively seeking out and considering different viewpoints, especially those that may be underrepresented or unheard in typical organizational processes.

An inclusive leader practices empathy and active listening by creating spaces where open, honest dialogue is encouraged, and where feedback is valued and acted upon. It's about recognizing and celebrating the unique contributions of each team member, understanding that a diverse team brings a wealth of experiences and insights that can lead to more innovative solutions.

Encouraging an Inclusive Culture

Create opportunities for team members to share their experiences and learn from each other through team-building activities, cultural exchange days, or regular informal gatherings.

Encourage open and honest communication through discussions about inclusivity and diversity, where team members can express their views and concerns. It's also important to have clear policies and practices that support inclusivity, such as equal opportunity policies and anti-discrimination guidelines.

Create opportunities for mentorship and career development for all team members, especially those from underrepresented groups, supplemented with training sessions that focus on topics like unconscious bias and cultural competency.

Leaders should lead by example, showing commitment to inclusivity in their actions and decisions and they should be approachable and open to feedback on how to improve the team's inclusivity.

Ethical Decision-Making

Establish a clear set of ethical principles to guide decisions, ensuring they are effective and ethically sound.

Training and Awareness

Educate the team both about the "what" and the "why" of ethical considerations through training programs that look into real-world ethical dilemmas faced in the industry and incorporate case studies, role-playing scenarios, and group discussions to make these sessions interactive and thought-provoking.

Push team members to stay informed about new developments in business ethics and create a forum for open discussion about ethical issues in the form of regular meetings or an online platform where team members can anonymously post questions or scenarios for discussion.

Ethical Dilemmas

Ethical decision-making involves being prepared to stand by your principles, even when it may be commercially challenging. Ethical dilemmas often arise when there are conflicting interests or values at play, including situations where business objectives might conflict with the best interests of users or the broader public. For example, a decision that maximizes profit in the short term might not align with long-term customer trust or environmental sustainability.

When dealing with such dilemmas, it is important to weigh the potential benefits against the ethical implications and to consider the impact on all stakeholders, including customers, employees, shareholders, and the community.

Push your team to think beyond the immediate consequences of decisions and consider the broader ethical implications by prioritizing customer privacy over aggressive marketing strategies, or choosing sustainable materials even if they are more costly. In my experience, maintaining integrity in difficult situations often leads to a stronger reputation for ethical conduct, which can become a key strength in the market.

Prioritizing Ethical Considerations

Evaluate the potential ethical implications of each choice and aim to make decisions that align with broader ethical standards by creating an ethics committee or a point person responsible for guiding ethical decisions. This group or individual can help assess the ethical dimensions of decisions, provide advice, and make sure that ethical considerations are consistently factored into the decision-making process.

You should also consider the long-term implications of decisions on stakeholders, the environment, and society at large to help make choices that are sustainable and responsible.

Conflict Resolution and Consensus Building

Conflict resolution is an essential skill for PMs, as it impacts the team's ability to work together effectively and reach optimal decisions. Conflict, when handled constructively, can lead to better understanding and innovative solutions. I learned that approaching conflicts with the intent to understand rather than to win often results in far more productive outcomes.

Create an environment where team members feel safe to express differing opinions without fear of retribution and setting ground rules for respectful communication and open dialogue.

When conflicts arise, address them promptly, use active listening to make sure all parties feel heard and understood and encourage team members to express their viewpoints and feelings without placing blame. Techniques such as "I" statements can be helpful in reducing defensiveness and focusing on problem-solving rather than personal attacks. In my experience, when team members feel genuinely listened to, it often diffuses tension and opens the door to constructive resolution.

Building consensus requires a balance between advocating for one's own position and being open to others' ideas. It's about finding a common ground that all team members can agree upon, even if it requires compromise from all sides. Use brainstorming sessions and round-table discussions to explore different options and their implications.

It's also important to recognize that consensus doesn't always mean complete agreement, and sometimes it's about reaching a decision that everyone can support or at least not oppose by prioritizing the collective goals of the team or project over individual preferences.

Emotional intelligence by Daniel Goleman is a great book that will help you better understand the viewpoints of your teammates when conflict arises.

Common Techniques to Solve Conflict—Active Listening

Practice sessions where team members paraphrase or summarize what others have said, to guarantee mutual understanding.

The exercise can start with one person speaking about a topic for a few minutes. After they finish, another team member summarizes or paraphrases what they heard to guarantee that the speaker is being heard accurately and also encourages listeners to pay close attention.

Such exercises can vary in complexity, from simple topics to more complex work-related issues with the goal to focus on the content of the message, the emotions behind it, and the underlying intentions.

Conflict Role-Playing

In this exercise, team members act out specific conflict scenarios in a controlled setting. These scenarios should be realistic and relevant to the challenges the team might face. During the role-play, one team member plays the role of the person initiating the conflict, while another plays the role of the person responding. The rest of the team can observe and provide feedback. This exercise allows team members to experience both sides of a conflict, encouraging empathy and understanding. After each role-play session, it's good to have a group discussion to reflect on the conflict management strategies used, what worked well, and what could be improved.

Consensus-Building Workshops

Consensus-building workshops are designed to improve the team's ability to reach agreements collaboratively. Team members are presented with scenarios that require a collective decision and they learn how to listen to differing viewpoints, find common ground, and negotiate mutually acceptable solutions. These workshops also often include training on conflict de-escalation techniques and how to manage group dynamics with the goal to equip team members with the tools and skills needed to build consensus in real-world situations.

Decision-Making Frameworks

Decision-making frameworks are methods that guide teams through the process of making decisions and help in organizing thoughts, considering various options, and assessing the implications of each choice.

Common frameworks include

- Pros and cons analysis: List the advantages and disadvantages of each option, helping to clarify the potential outcomes of different choices.

- Six thinking hats: Developed by Edward de Bono, this method encourages looking at a decision from multiple perspectives, such as emotional, analytical, creative, and more. Each "hat" represents a different style of thinking.

- SWOT analysis: SWOT helps teams assess different options in the context of internal and external factors.

Conflict Resolution Policy

A conflict resolution policy outlines how conflicts within the team should be addressed and resolved and typically includes the steps to be taken when a conflict arises, the roles and responsibilities of those involved in the resolution process, and guidelines for fair and respectful communication.

The policy should encourage an environment where conflicts are seen as opportunities for growth, rather than as disruptions, including procedures for informal resolution, like open discussions or mediation by a third party, as well as more formal procedures if needed.

Having a clear conflict resolution policy helps all team members understand how to navigate disagreements effectively and respectfully, encouraging a healthy and collaborative work environment.

SIX THINKING HATS

The "six thinking hats" method, developed by Edward de Bono, is a powerful tool for decision-making and problem-solving within teams.

Each "hat" represents a different perspective:

- White Hat (Information): Focuses on data and facts. Example: Analyzing customer feedback data to understand their preferences.

- Red Hat (Emotions): Looks at problems using intuition and emotions. Example: Gauging team morale and motivation regarding a project change.

- Black Hat (Judgment): Critical thinking, looking at the cons. Example: Assessing potential risks in a new product feature.

- Yellow Hat (Optimism): Positive perspective, exploring the benefits. Example: Identifying the potential success and benefits of a marketing strategy.

- Green Hat (Creativity): Creative and alternative solutions. Example: Brainstorming innovative features to solve user pain points.

- Blue Hat (Process Control): Managing and organizing the thinking process. Example: Overseeing the meeting flow and ensuring all perspectives are covered.

Using these hats, teams can explore issues from multiple angles, leading to more thorough and balanced decision-making.

Leadership Development

Leadership development is important for sustaining the long-term success and health of a team or organization. With this process you identify individuals within the team who have the potential to grow into future leaders. These are often individuals who excel in their current roles and also demonstrate key leadership qualities such as effective communication, strategic thinking, and a strong alignment with the team's vision and goals.

Once potential leaders are identified, it's important to invest in their development through different initiatives.

Mentorship Programs

Mentorship programs are a key element in leadership development as they offer opportunities for potential leaders to get insights from more experienced colleagues. I've found that pairing the right mentor with a mentee can dramatically accelerate the mentee's growth. You need to identify mentors who are not only skilled and experienced but also exhibit strong leadership qualities and a commitment to nurturing others' growth.

The process of pairing mentors with mentees should be thoughtful, considering each mentee's specific developmental needs and the strengths of the mentors.

Setting clear objectives and expectations for the mentorship is important, including focusing on certain skill areas, expanding professional knowledge, or working toward specific career goals. Mentees should also feel comfortable discussing their career aspirations and challenges, while mentors should provide guidance and feedback.

Leadership Training Workshops

Leadership training workshops are specialized programs designed to equip potential leaders with the necessary skills and knowledge for effective leadership and often cover a range of topics, including planning, team management, conflict resolution, communication, and decision-making.

To maximize their impact, workshops should be interactive and involve role-playing exercises, case study analyses, group discussions, and problem-solving activities to help participants apply theoretical concepts to real-world scenarios.

Workshops can also include sessions led by experienced leaders who share their insights and provide participants with first-hand knowledge of the challenges and rewards of leadership.

Rotational Assignments

Offering opportunities to work in different roles or departments can help leaders understand various aspects of the organization and develop a more holistic perspective.

Identify roles that offer learning experiences and align with the employee's career path and choose assignments that will push the individual out of their comfort zone. During these assignments, employees should be given real responsibilities and projects, allowing them to apply their skills in new contexts and gain practical experience.

Project Leadership Opportunities

Allowing people to lead projects or initiatives gives them practical experience and a chance to demonstrate their skills. In my experience, these opportunities are an excellent way for potential leaders to gain confidence in their leadership capabilities.

To implement this effectively, identify projects that align with each team member's strengths and leadership development goals and are challenging enough to stretch their abilities, but also achievable with the resources and support available.

As these team members take on project leadership roles, provide them with the necessary support and guidance like regular check-ins, access to additional resources, or mentorship from experienced leaders with the goal to create a supportive environment where they can experiment, learn, and grow.

Encourage these aspiring leaders to take full ownership of their projects, including planning, team coordination, problem-solving, and decision-making.

After the project's completion, discuss what went well, what challenges were encountered, and what could be improved to help prepare them for larger leadership roles in the future.

In tandem with developing future leaders, you should also work on succession plans to make sure that there are always qualified individuals ready to take on leadership roles when they become available.

This involves

- Understanding future needs

- Developing a talent pipeline

- Transition planning

- Feedback and evaluation

Understanding Future Needs

Analyze trends within your industry and changes in the market to get insights into the future your organization will operate in and the type of leadership that will be needed to navigate it successfully.

Work with current leaders and stakeholders to understand their perspectives on future challenges and opportunities and get inputs on the qualities and competencies future leaders will need to have. Consider the organizational culture and values, and how these might evolve as future leaders will need to embody and promote these values, so understanding how they align with the direction of the company is important.

Once you have a clear picture of the future needs, you can start aligning your leadership development initiatives accordingly, adjusting your criteria for selecting potential leaders, the focus of your training programs, and the experiences you provide to future leaders.

Transition Planning

It's important to guarantee a smooth handover when a new leader steps into a role, including clearly defining the roles and responsibilities of the new position. Understanding what the role entails helps both the incoming leader and the team to adjust to the change more effectively. Preparation may include briefing sessions where the incoming leader can learn about the team's current projects, goals, and challenges.

During this transition keep the team informed about changes in leadership and timelines to help manage expectations and reduce uncertainty. It's important to frame these transitions positively, highlighting the opportunities they bring.

Mentoring or coaching during the transition phase can provide additional support to the new leader with ongoing guidance from the outgoing leader or support from other senior members of the organization.

Evaluation

Assess the progress of potential leaders to make sure they are on track to meet the demands of future leadership roles and create a regular feedback system like performance reviews and 360-degree feedback, where input is collected from supervisors, peers, and direct reports.

In addition to formal evaluations, you can also use informal feedback through ongoing dialogue between potential leaders and their mentors or supervisors which offer timely, specific feedback that is crucial for growth.

Another aspect of this process is self-assessment as potential leaders should reflect on their own performance and development as it helps individuals understand their own progress and identify areas where they need more support or training. It's also important to align feedback and evaluations with the specific competencies and skills required for future leadership roles.

CHAPTER 7

Current and Future Trends in Product Management

We now approach the final stop of our journey—this chapter is an exploration of the current and emerging trends reshaping the product field.

We'll explore the latest methodologies that are currently shaping the world of product management and analyze how these elements influence user experiences today.

We'll also look toward the future, speculating on the direction of this discipline. How will continuous advancements in tech, such as augmented reality or blockchain, redefine the role of product managers? What new challenges and opportunities will arise as consumer behaviors and market landscapes change?

As before, while we focus on the role of the product manager, the insights in this chapter may be valuable to anyone involved in product development, marketing, business strategy, or leadership roles.

Topics in this chapter:

1. **Embracing AI and Machine Learning:** Understand how artificial intelligence and machine learning are revolutionizing product management, from data analysis to automated customer interactions.

© Michele Galli 2025
M. Galli, *Navigating the Product Galaxy*, https://doi.org/10.1007/979-8-8688-1148-7_7

2. **The Rise of Remote Product Teams:** Explore the challenges and strategies for managing and collaborating with remote product teams in a digitally connected world.

3. **Sustainability in Product Development:** Explore the growing importance of sustainability and how it's becoming a crucial part of product development and strategy.

4. **Predicting the Future:** Look at future trends in product management, including potential technological advancements and changes in consumer behavior.

Embracing AI and Machine Learning

The integration of Artificial Intelligence and Machine Learning is reshaping the very fabric of how products are conceived, developed, and optimized. These technologies represent a big change as they offer new ways to understand and respond to market and customer dynamics.

These are no longer futuristic concepts; they are integral parts of our current business environment and it's important for PMs to stay on top of these developments, but it's also important to note that these advancements are relevant to many other roles within an organization, including CEOs, marketing teams, and other stakeholders.

With AI, enormous amounts of data become navigable, showing patterns and insights that were previously hidden in the complexity of market behaviors and consumer trends which allow product managers to make decisions that are data-driven and aligned with the needs and behaviors of customers.

The automation capabilities of AI are also revolutionizing the traditional tasks within product management. Daily, repetitive tasks are transformed into automated processes, allowing product managers to focus their talents and energies on strategic thinking and innovation.

Machine Learning, on the other hand, brings a self-evolving aspect to product management as services can now continuously improve and adapt, learning from every interaction and feedback loop, ensuring offerings stay relevant and fine-tuned to the consumer desires.

However, embracing these technologies is not without its challenges as it requires product managers to continuously update their knowledge and skills, staying on top of the latest developments and understanding how to apply them effectively. Another challenge is finding the right balance between thoughtfully exploring ways to apply AI to products versus the temptation to experimenting with AI features in an ad hoc manner without a strategic intent. This often results in wasted resources and features that lack cohesion with the broader product strategy. Instead, you should identify the specific problems AI can solve, plan for a well-defined use case, and make sure that each AI initiative aligns with user needs and business goals.

Looking forward, the potential of AI and ML in product management is huge. These technologies promise to unlock new levels of personalization, efficiency, and market understanding and they hold the key to better products and to more insightful and responsive product development strategies.

AI-Driven Market Analysis Techniques

AI-driven techniques are revolutionizing the way we understand and respond to market dynamics as they use the power of AI to dig deeper into market data, offering insights that were previously inaccessible. I'm quite excited about the future possibilities that these advancements will bring, as they will likely redefine what is possible in product management.

One of the most impactful techniques is sentiment analysis on social media. By using natural language processing, product managers can scan vast amounts of social media content to understand the public opinion about their products and brands.

Another powerful application of AI in market analysis is predictive analytics. By examining patterns in historical data, AI algorithms can forecast future market trends, consumer behaviors, and potential shifts in demand.

AI algorithms also bring a new level of sophistication to customer segmentation. By analyzing various customer data points, AI can uncover distinct customer groups based on multiple criteria such as behavior, preferences, and demographics and enable product managers to tailor their strategies more precisely, ensuring that products and marketing efforts resonate with the right audience.

Competitive analysis is another area where AI makes a significant impact. AI tools can monitor competitors, tracking changes in pricing, new product launches, and marketing strategies.

Machine Learning for Customer Feedback

Machine Learning is reshaping the way product managers interpret and act on customer feedback. The traditional approach to customer feedback often involves manually going through comments, reviews, and surveys—a process that is time-consuming and subject to human error and bias. ML revolutionizes this by applying algorithms that can quickly analyze and categorize feedback at scale. These algorithms are trained to recognize patterns, sentiments, and even specific issues or suggestions within the feedback.

For example, ML can categorize feedback into themes such as usability issues, feature requests, or customer service experiences, helping product managers identify common pain points. Also, sentiment analysis tools powered by ML can assess the emotional tone of the feedback, distinguishing between positive, negative, and neutral sentiments to provide a clearer understanding of customer satisfaction.

Another significant advantage of ML is its ability to track changes in customer feedback over time. By analyzing trends in the data, ML can highlight whether changes made to a product are positively impacting customer satisfaction.

AI-Powered Personalization

In today's market, where customer expectations are higher than ever, personalization has become a key differentiator, with AI leveraging data from user interactions, preferences, and behaviors to create a unique experience for each user. By analyzing this data, AI algorithms can tailor the user interface, content, and recommendations to match individual user needs and make sure that users are presented with options most relevant to them, improving their overall experience.

For example, an AI-driven personalization system in an e-commerce platform can suggest products based on a user's browsing history, purchase patterns, and even social media activity. In a content streaming service, AI can curate a list of shows or music tailored to the user's past viewing or listening habits. This makes the user experience more engaging and helps in building brand loyalty and increasing user retention.

Also, AI-powered personalization adapts in real time as a user's preferences evolve, so does the personalized experience and keeps the user experience fresh and relevant, consistently meeting or exceeding user expectations.

Ethical Considerations in AI

Incorporating AI into product management requires to go deep into several ethical dimensions, from data privacy to AI transparency. As a PM and leader, you will need understanding of ethical principles in AI, not just for legal compliance but for encouraging trust and integrity in your products.

Data privacy in AI transcends legal obligations and involves an ethical commitment to protecting user data, which requires a data management strategy that includes data collection, storage, and usage practices. Such strategy should be transparent to users, providing them clarity and control over their data with regular updates to privacy policies, user education on data usage, and security measures to prevent breaches.

Addressing biases in AI algorithms is another complex layer. You will need to identify potential biases in data sets and guarantee that AI systems are trained on representative data sets, including involving multidisciplinary teams in the development process to bring in different perspectives and mitigate biases.

The Rise of Remote Product Teams

Post COVID, remote and hybrid teams have become the norm, making it essential for product managers to master the art of managing these setups effectively. Ensuring productivity in remote teams requires addressing several key aspects to create an efficient workflow.

Clear Communication

If you want to have good communication across your remote team, schedule regular video meetings to connect on a personal level for better team cohesion. It's also important to maintain a central repository of key decisions, minutes from meetings, and action items in shared digital spaces like Google Docs as it helps keep everyone aligned.

You should have clear communication guidelines to articulate the preferred communication channels for different scenarios, establish rules around response times, and set expectations for after-hours communication. In my experience, having these guidelines in place is particularly important for remote teams, as it helps prevent burnout and supports a healthy work–life balance.

Cultivating a Remote Team Culture

Create an environment where team members feel connected and valued despite physical distances by implementing regular virtual team-building activities that go beyond work-related discussions, such as online social events or virtual coffee breaks.

Recognize and celebrate team achievements and milestones to build a sense of community and promote work–life balance as much as possible. It's also important to empower team members with the freedom to manage their tasks and time as it can lead to increased motivation and productivity. I've learned that when team members have control over their schedules, they're often more committed to delivering high-quality work.

Navigating Time Zone Differences

Establish core hours and maximize overlaps across time zones to create a window for meetings or collaborative work sessions and use scheduling tools that account for everyone's time zone.

Support asynchronous work as much as possible to allow team members to contribute according to their own schedules, but for important meetings that require live attendance, make sure to rotate meeting times to avoid one single group to be consistently at a disadvantage. You can also record these meetings to support inclusivity and allow team members to stay informed regardless of their geographic location.

Sustainability in Product Development

Sustainability signifies a transformative change toward integrating eco-friendly practices at every stage of the product life cycle, from selecting sustainable materials, to optimizing for energy efficiency during production, and considering the environmental impact of products from conception to disposal.

This focus resonates with the growing consumer demand for environmentally conscious products and also aligns with global objectives aimed at reducing ecological footprints. By prioritizing sustainability, companies can elevate their brand reputation, access new markets driven by green consumerism, and create innovation in eco-friendly product design and development.

Product managers, in this context, are tasked with ensuring that the ethos of environmental responsibility is reflected in the end product and in the methodologies and processes that bring the product to life.

This journey toward sustainability represents a fundamental rethinking of how products are developed, with an eye on long-term environmental stewardship and social responsibility.

Life Cycle Assessment (LCA)

An LCA evaluates the environmental impacts of a product throughout its entire life cycle, from raw material extraction to disposal, and helps in identifying areas where improvements can be made to reduce environmental footprint.

This process involves collecting data on the energy and resources consumed and the waste and emissions produced at each stage of the product's life. By analyzing this data, product managers can make informed decisions on materials selection, design changes, and manufacturing processes to improve sustainability. Implementing an LCA requires a commitment to data collection and a willingness to reevaluate and adjust product strategies based on findings.

Sustainable Sourcing

Where possible you should procure materials and services in a way that minimizes environmental impact while supporting social and ethical practices and evaluate suppliers based on their environmental performance, labor practices, and overall sustainability policies.

Implementing sustainable sourcing requires developing criteria for selecting suppliers, promoting transparency in the supply chain, and encouraging suppliers to adopt greener practices to reduce the environmental footprint of products and improve the brand reputation and customer trust.

Design for Sustainability

Design products with minimal environmental impact throughout their life cycle and incorporate sustainable materials, energy efficiency, and recyclability into the design process. DfS aims to reduce resource consumption and waste generation, extending product life and facilitating end-of-life management. This approach requires a shift in traditional design thinking, prioritizing environmental considerations alongside functionality and aesthetics.

Energy Efficiency

You should also think on how to minimize energy consumption throughout a product's life, from manufacturing to end user operation, optimize product design and use energy-efficient components and materials. Energy efficiency reduces environmental impact and lowers costs for both manufacturers and consumers by employing innovative technologies and design principles that improve the product functionality while consuming less energy.

Packaging Innovations

You can reduce the environmental impact also through the use of recyclable materials, minimizing packaging size and weight, and employing biodegradable options to lessen waste in landfills and reduce the carbon footprint associated with the production and disposal of packaging. By integrating design principles that prioritize sustainability, companies can significantly decrease the ecological impact of their products while meeting consumer demand for environmentally responsible packaging.

Consumer Engagement

Engaging consumers in sustainability means educating them on the environmental impact of their purchases and encouraging sustainable consumption behaviors through communication about the sustainability efforts embedded in your product development, packaging, and life cycle. Additionally, you can leverage online platforms for storytelling about sustainability initiatives, and can offer incentives for consumers to choose sustainable options.

Predicting the Future

As we look beyond the current landscape of product management and technology, our responsibility as leaders is to predict the future and guide the teams that navigate the complexities of product development. This final step into the unknown requires us to use every tool, insight, and lesson learned from our journey so far.

The acceleration of tech innovation continues to reshape the field of product management as AI and Machine Learning are redefining what's possible, offering unprecedented insights into customer behaviors. The integration of these technologies into product management tools will enable predictive analytics, automate decision-making processes, and personalize user experiences at scale. Additionally, the Internet of Things and 5G connectivity are further blurring the lines between physical and digital products, creating new opportunities for innovation in product functionality and user engagement.

AI and Machine Learning

As we said at the beginning of this chapter, AI and ML tools are offering product managers the tools to predict user behaviors, automate routine tasks, and personalize user experiences at an unprecedented scale. These technologies enable the analysis of massive datasets to uncover patterns and insights that were previously inaccessible, driving more informed decision-making and planning. In my opinion, the future advancements in AI and ML will likely introduce autonomous systems capable of making optimization decisions in real time, which will further revolutionize product management.

Augmented Reality and Virtual Reality

AR and VR technologies are transforming user experiences by bridging the gap between the digital and physical worlds. Product managers can leverage AR and VR to create immersive and interactive experiences that increase product engagement, whether it's through virtual product demonstrations, interactive training modules, or better customer service interactions.

Internet of Things

The proliferation of IoT devices is turning everyday objects into sources of valuable data. For product managers, this opens up new ways for creating interconnected products that integrate into users' lives. The challenge will be to manage the complexity of these ecosystems, ensuring security, privacy, and ease of use.

Blockchain Technology

While often associated with cryptocurrencies, blockchain holds significant potential for product management in areas such as supply chain transparency, data security, and digital identity verification. By enabling secure, decentralized transactions and data sharing, blockchains can facilitate new business models and trust mechanisms, particularly in products that require high levels of security or involve complex transactions.

Consumer Behavior Shifts

As technology evolves, so too does the consumer. Tomorrow's users will demand more personalized, engaging, and ethical interactions with the products they use. I've seen a clear trend toward consumers aligning their spending with their values, which requires product managers to adopt a more holistic view of the user experience, one that considers both individual life style impacts and broader societal effects.

Sustainability and ethical considerations will move from side concerns to central components of product strategy, as consumers increasingly align their spending with their values. Today's consumers are more inclined to favor products that demonstrate environmental conservation, ethical sourcing, and transparency throughout the product life cycle.

Consumers now demand personalization at an unprecedented level, expecting products and services to serve their preferences, behaviors, and values, which shows the importance of leveraging advanced data analytics and AI to create experiences that resonate on a personal level while maintaining a delicate balance with privacy concerns.

The value placed on community and social connection has risen, with consumers seeking products that encourage a sense of belonging. In my view, creating products that build and support communities will become an increasingly important aspect of product management.

Consumers are also increasingly more attracted to experiential consumption, where the emphasis changes from owning products to experiencing outcomes which requires product managers to think beyond traditional boundaries, creating services and ecosystems that improve life styles and offer meaningful experiences.

Agile and Beyond

The methodologies that guide product development will continue to evolve. While Agile has set the standard for flexibility, the future will see the rise of even more adaptive frameworks, which will need to accommodate distributed teams and asynchronous work patterns. Product managers will need to become skilled at leading across borders and cultures, encouraging innovation in a truly global context.

The journey from agile methodologies to the horizons beyond represents a change in how teams conceptualize, develop, and deliver products. It's clear that the principles guiding us need to evolve even further to accommodate the increasing complexity of product ecosystems, the diversity of global teams, and the changes in technology and consumer expectations.

The next evolution in product development methodologies will likely build on agile's foundations but extend into more adaptive, fluid practices that can better accommodate remote work and will prioritize the speed and responsiveness of agile but also the resilience and sustainability of product development processes. They will encourage product managers and their teams to think beyond the confines of traditional development cycles, embracing a more holistic view of the product life cycle.

Cultural and organizational adaptability will also become increasingly important. As product teams navigate the challenges of global collaboration, the methodologies of the future will need to support diversity, equity, and inclusion, to make sure that diverse perspectives are welcomed and seen as essential to the creative and problem-solving processes. This will encourage innovation and resilience, enabling teams to draw on a wide range of experiences and insights as they develop products that meet the needs of a global user base.

The Role of Data

In the future, data will become an even more important asset. However, with the proliferation of data sources, the challenge will change from data collection to interpretation. Product managers will need to develop sophisticated data literacy skills, enabling them to recognize signals from noise and apply insights in real time.

Privacy and data protection will also become more complex, requiring managers to navigate regulations and ethical considerations.

Predictive analytics and real-time decision-making will become the norm. Product managers will increasingly rely on data to forecast user needs, market changes, and technology trends, enabling proactive rather than reactive strategies. This shift toward proactive management, in my view, will allow for the anticipation of user issues before they arise and the identification of new market opportunities as they emerge.

The ethical considerations surrounding data will also come to the forefront as product managers must also address concerns related to privacy, security, and data governance and they will need to make sure there is transparency in how data is collected, used, and protected to maintain trust and comply with increasingly stringent regulatory requirements.

A Few Final Words

Finally, the most important tool in predicting and shaping the future will be a mindset of continuous learning. A theme we kept coming back to throughout this book.

Product managers must remain voracious learners, staying on top of emerging trends, technologies, and methodologies. Cultivating a culture of curiosity and resilience within their teams will help them navigate the uncertainties of the future.

The essence of learning in product management rests in the relentless pursuit of knowledge, skills, and insights that can drive better product decisions, create better user experiences, and improve team dynamics.

Adaptation, on the other hand, is the ability to apply these learnings to pivot strategies, processes, and products in response to new information and changing environments. It means being prepared to question assumptions, re-evaluate goals, and experiment with new approaches. Product managers and their teams must remain flexible and resilient, ready to navigate through the uncertainties of product development.

Creating a culture that supports learning requires intentional efforts and involves setting up systems and processes that encourage experimentation, feedback, and reflection.

Pushing team members to set aside time for learning activities, participate in industry conferences, and engage in cross-functional collaboration can spark innovation and creativity. Similarly, adopting a fail-fast mentality, where failures are seen as opportunities for learning rather than setbacks, can cultivate an environment where adaptation is part of the DNA.

As we look beyond, the future of product management is a horizon filled with potential. Embrace change, innovation, and remain committed to understand and meet the needs of your customers so that as a product manager you can not only predict the future but also play a hand in creating it.

Appendix

Notes

Some names, company names, and case studies have been changed and adapted to maintain the privacy of the individuals and organizations involved.

Other case studies have been created to showcase practical examples of the product techniques.

Works Cited

Brown, Tim, and Barry Kātz. *Change by Design: How Design Thinking Transforms Organizations and Inspires Innovation.* HarperCollins, 2009. Accessed 13 August 2024.

Cooper, Alan. *The Inmates are Running the Asylum.* Sams, 2004. Accessed 13 August 2024.

Cooper, Alan, et al. *About Face: The Essentials of Interaction Design.* Wiley, 2014. Accessed 13 August 2024.

Doran, George T. "There's a S.M.A.R.T. Way to Write Management's Goals and Objectives."

Duvall, Paul M., et al. *Continuous Integration: Improving Software Quality and Reducing Risk.* Addison-Wesley, 2007. Accessed 13 August 2024.

Goleman, Daniel. *Emotional Intelligence: Why It Can Matter More Than IQ.* Random House Publishing Group, 2005. Accessed 13 August 2024.

© Michele Galli 2025
M. Galli, *Navigating the Product Galaxy*, https://doi.org/10.1007/979-8-8688-1148-7

Humble, Jez, and David Farley. *Continuous Delivery: Reliable Software Releases Through Build, Test, and Deployment Automation*. Pearson Education, 2010. Accessed 13 August 2024.

Humphrey, Albert. "SWOT Analysis for Management Consulting."

Kim, Gene, et al. *The DevOps Handbook: How to Create World-class Agility, Reliability, and Security in Technology Organizations*. IT Revolution Press, 2016. Accessed 13 August 2024.

Kniberg, Henrik, and Mattias Skarin. *Kanban and Scrum: Making the Most of Both*. C4Media Incorporated, 2010. Accessed 13 August 2024.

Michalko, Michael. *Creative Thinkering: Putting Your Imagination to Work*. New World Library, 2011. Accessed 13 August 2024.

Moore, Geoffrey A. *Crossing the Chasm: Marketing and Selling Disruptive Products to Mainstream Customers*. HarperCollins, 2002. Accessed 13 August 2024.

Murchison, Julian M. *Ethnography Essentials: Designing, Conducting, and Presenting Your Research*. Wiley, 2010. Accessed 13 August 2024.

Noriaki, Kano. "Attractive quality and must-be quality." *The Journal of Japanese Society for Quality Control*, 1984.

Osterwalder, Alexander, et al. *Value Proposition Design: How to Create Products and Services Customers Want*. Wiley, 2014. Accessed 13 August 2024.

Patton, Jeff, and Peter Economy. *User Story Mapping: Discover the Whole Story, Build the Right Product*. Edited by Peter Economy, O'Reilly, 2014. Accessed 13 August 2024.

Porter, Michael E. *Competitive Strategy: Techniques for Analyzing Industries and Competitors*. Free Press, 1998. Accessed 13 August 2024.

Reichheld, Frederick F. *The Ultimate Question 2.0: How Net Promoter Companies Thrive in a Customer-Driven World*. Harvard Business Review Press, 2011.

Sutherland, Jeff, and J.J. Sutherland. *Scrum: The Art of Doing Twice the Work in Half the Time*. Crown, 2014. Accessed 13 August 2024.

Index

M. Galli, *Navigating the Product Galaxy*, https://doi.org/10.1007/979-8-8688-1148-7

Printed in the United States
by Baker & Taylor Publisher Services